CULT WRITERS

CULT WRITERS

50 Nonconformist Novelists You Need to Know

IAN HAYDN SMITH

WHITE LION
PUBLISHING

CONTENTS

INTRODUCTION

—

The notion of a cult writer is a slippery one, not only in defining the parameters of the term, but also in understanding the transient nature of it. Time can transform a cult novel into a classic, but a classic novel can also attain cult status with the passage of time. As this volume features only fifty entries, how is it possible to represent the vast landscape of books – a world in which tens of thousands are published every year – and those who write them?

The road that led to this book began with a series of crossroads, decisions made that set the parameters of what it would be. The primary focus would be novelists, although some – most notably Joan Didion – would be equally acclaimed for their non-fiction work or, as in the case of Jean Genet, Eve Babitz, Charles Bukowski and Chris Kraus, have built a writing career out of transforming their own experiences into a fictional hybrid. The second decision was to limit the selection to authors published in this or the last century. That still leaves a question mark over what exactly constitutes a cult writer.

In the preface to his 1992 publication *Classic Cult Fiction: A Companion to Popular Cult Literature*, Thomas Reed Whissen writes that Goethe's *The Sorrows of Young Werther* was the first cult book published, as it set out 'all the elements that have come to characterize cult literature'. He continues:

Regardless of plot or setting, characters or time periods, symbols or themes, all cult books have elements of romantic hope and longing as well as romantic disillusion and melancholy. They dream of a different, usually better, world – or they warn against the direction they see the world heading. Entertainment, amusement, diversion, distraction – these are not their goals. They expect, they invite, they demand response. For

this reason, they usually have few neutral readers. One either rejects them as trivial or boring or falls under their spell and becomes a cult follower.

Further to this, an article written for the American Library Association Journals highlights the importance of the reader in the process of identifying a cult work. It is not just the themes of a book that define it as cult – it is the response to them. As such, many works have attained this status as a result of the fervour of their readership, which can be a specific group in society, such as adolescents. Themes of alienation, displacement and vulnerability have the power to hold sway over readers who identify with a character that doesn't fit easily into the world around them.

Another element of the work by the writers who appear in this book is their relationship to genre. It's not that these writers don't work within a given genre, but that they appear more comfortable transgressing the boundaries of any category, or melding various genres to create a hybrid that better reflects their interests. (Even the more 'literary' writers in this selection are celebrated for their experimentation with form.) Kathy Acker, J.G. Ballard, Octavia E. Butler, Philip K. Dick, Ursula K. Le Guin, Doris Lessing, the Strugatsky brothers and Kurt Vonnegut are all renowned -- and acclaimed – writers in the field of speculative or science fiction. Italo Calvino and Angela Carter have embraced classical fables. Cormac McCarthy has taken on the myth of the American West. Jean Genet and Jim Thompson tackle the criminal world, while J.R.R. Tolkien conjures up a fantasy universe. Charles Bukowski, William Burroughs, Denis Johnson, Ken Kesey and Irvine Welsh journey into the lives of alcoholics and drug addicts. And the exploration of erotic desire has formed the basis of works by Kathy Acker, Marguerite Duras, Jean Genet, Anaïs Nin, Pauline Réage and Jean Rhys. For each, genre is more a point of embarkation than an area of residence.

These writers have achieved cult status because of their unwillingness to conform to the strictures of any given genre. Sylvia Plath's *The Bell Jar* (1963) might present a compelling portrait of teen life, but equally important is the book's approach to issues surrounding mental illness, and the role and expectations placed on women at the time it was written. The best work by Jim Thompson didn't so much transcend crime fiction as push it to its farthest reaches. *The Killer Inside Me* (1952) remains an extraordinary journey into the mind of a psychopath and a chilling examination of the nature of violence. This is also a theme that appears in the work of Kathy Acker, Albert Camus, Jean Genet and Cormac McCarthy. Their approach might differ, but for each the character of the outsider plays a pivotal role.

However, for all its focus on their work, this book is ultimately about the creators. Which raises another question: is a cult writer defined by the work they produce or the life they have lived? As you will glean from the portraits included here, the answer is: both. More specifically, it depends on the life lived in the external or internal world of a writer. Outside of a youth existing in a Japanese internment camp, as detailed in *Empire of the Sun* (1984) and his memoir *Miracles of Life* (2008), and his time as a pilot recounted in *The Kindness of Women*

(1991), J.G. Ballard spent the majority of his life residing in the suburbs of London. There was little in his everyday existence beyond the pale of essential domestic activity. But the landscape of this world proved a powerful catalyst in the creation of his most disturbing fiction. By contrast, Charles Bukowski's alcoholism, work life and relationships pretty much wrote themselves onto the pages of *Post Office* (1971), *Factotum* (1975) and *Tales of Ordinary Madness* (1983). And Janet Frame's *An Angel at My Table* (1984) might have represented her autobiographical work, but if her fiction veered further afield it still drew on her own troubled experiences.

Cult fiction is not the preserve of male, white or English-language writers. This book is an attempt to encompass a wide spectrum of novelists. Female writers account for twenty-three of the figures chosen. The US accounts for the same number of entries. Eleven are from mainland Europe (Marguerite Duras was born in French-occupied Vietnam and Michel Houellebecq on the Indian Ocean island of Réunion, but both are recognized as French writers), while five are British. There are two entries apiece from Japan, Russia and what is now the Czech Republic, and one entry each for Algeria, Guadeloupe, New Zealand, Mexico and Argentina. (Although he was born and died in Europe, Julio Cortázar is regarded as an Argentine writer.)

There will always be omissions with a book like this. In particular, some might feel certain categories are under-represented. Yet these profiles not only introduce a key figure, they can stand as representative of a certain type or movement of fiction. William Burroughs, for instance, is one of the quintessential Beat writers. As such, he also represents Jack Kerouac. Even if their style of writing is markedly different, they hail from the same creative group. Zora Neale Hurston could have been joined by fellow Harlem Renaissance icon Langston Hughes. Thomas Pynchon stands in for other experimental writers such as William Gaddis, Roberto Bolaño and David Foster Wallace, just as Virginia Woolf represents the Bloomsbury Group and the Modernist writers who emerged in the early decades of the 20th century. J.R.R. Tolkien might be the most mainstream writer here, but his cult status has grown over the years, reaching global proportions now. But a larger selection could have also included a wide range of writers, from Mervyn Peake to Nnedi Okorafor. Likewise, both speculative and crime fiction present a taste of a vast landscape of writers that run the gamut from Aldous Huxley and Anne McCaffrey to William Gibson and Chen Qiufan, and Georges Simenon and Patricia Highsmith to Walter Mosley and James Sallis.

This volume could also have welcomed Louis-Ferdinand Céline, George S. Schuyler, L. Ron Hubbard, Richard Wright, Colin Wilson, Harper Lee, Amos Tutuola, Xi Xi, William Melvin Kelley, Ann Quin, Joseph Heller, Erica Jong, B.S. Johnson, Luke Rhinehart, Wang Xiaobo, Katherine Dunn, Chuck Palahniuk, Mark Z. Danielewski, Hawa Jande Golakai and Natsuo Kirino, to name countless others.

It could be argued that many, if not all, the writers featured in this volume are part of a canon. They may not all make literary critic Harold Bloom's list of giants (one whose focus was almost entirely West-facing), but their status has shifted from cult outlier to a place closer to the heart of the literary establishment. Times are changing and so should this list. The number of translated books available is on the increase – both via specialist and mainstream publishing houses. They present a multiplicity of worlds and perspectives to their readership, which will hopefully increase appetites and in doing so transform what constitutes a great book. Some might see this as the marginalization of certain cultural traditions. Better to see it as an opportunity to enjoy the richness of fiction from all corners of the world. And in a decade or two, when someone returns to the idea of cult writers, their selection will likely be very different from the one you are to read here.

KATHY ACKER (1947-1997)

—— THE PUNK FEMINIST

Influenced by Marguerite Duras, William Burroughs and Alain Robbe-Grillet, Kathy Acker created post-modern fiction that grew out of the punk movement in the late 1970s.

Born Karen Lehman, Acker did not know her father, Donald, who absconded before her birth. Her relationship with Claire, her mother, was fractious – her mother blaming her husband's departure on the imminent arrival of their child – until a few years before Claire's suicide in 1978. That relationship fuelled Acker's rebelliousness and would inform much of her writing, particularly her 1993 book *My Mother: Demonology*, with its portrait of a woman coming to terms with her past. Raised in a culturally but not religiously Jewish family on Manhattan's well-to-do Upper East Side, Acker would later express her indifference towards her heritage. Her spiritual home lay in the future, and downtown, in the city's East Village.

In the late 1960s, Acker studied poetry and literature at the University of California, San Diego. Around that time, she created a limited series of chapbooks that were mailed to key cultural figures of the era, positioning her on the rapidly changing map of the US art world. She married Robert Acker in 1966, but the relationship ended some years later and was followed by a short-lived marriage to the experimental composer Peter Gordon. However, throughout her adult life Acker identified as bisexual.

Her first book, *Politics*, was published in 1972. She became a key figure in the nascent punk scene. There was little money in her creative endeavours, so she supported herself with jobs that ranged from clerical work to performing as a stripper and appearing in pornographic films. She cemented her reputation with *The Childlike Life of the Black Tarantula By the Black Tarantula* (1973). It set the tone of her work, which embraced the aesthetics of the Nouveau Roman, rejecting the conventions of classical fiction in favour of experimentation. She would

plagiarize in some style, as evinced by her *Great Expectations* (1983) and *Don Quixote* (1986), or through her lifting from Nathaniel Hawthorne's *The Scarlet Letter* (1850) for her *Blood and Guts in High School* (1984) and Mark Twain for *Empire of the Senseless* (1988). Like Burroughs, she revelled in cut-up techniques to challenge the flow of narrative and to inspire new artistic avenues, and celebrated sexuality with a rawness that recalled Duras and Jean Genet. Her style was combative, challenging gender stereotypes, but sex positive, finding in pornography a release that countered the work of some feminist peers. As Burroughs put it, 'Acker gives her work the power to mirror the reader's soul.'

In 1979, Acker's short story 'New York City in 1979' won the Pushcart Prize, which raised her profile further. She moved to London in 1984, just as her early work was being republished and selling out. Her public readings/performances were always an important part of her work, which she continued to pursue while moving between the US and UK in the last decade of her life. Her influence is wide, evinced by Chris Kraus's critical biography *After Kathy Acker* (2017); Olivia Laing's referencing of her in her novel *Crudo* (2018); and her friend Neil Gaiman immortalizing her in comic book format as Delerium, one of The Endless in the Sandman series.

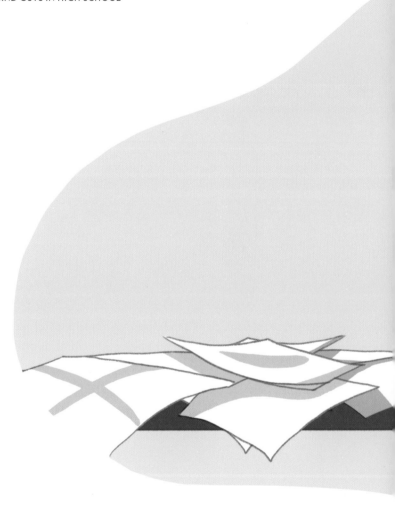

PAIN IS THE WORLD. I DON'T HAVE ANYWHERE TO RUN.

BLOOD AND GUTS IN HIGH SCHOOL

EVE BABITZ (1943)

—— THE 'IT' WRITER

Eve Babitz drew from her own life to write a series of books chronicling life in and around Hollywood.

Babitz's tales of Los Angeles life in the 1950s, 60s and 70s are ribald, lively and populated with characters who not only feel as though they've come straight out of a film, many of them actually did. Her synthesis of fiction and memoir brings her home town to life as a 'realm of the self-enchanted which was once, briefly, more devastating than Caesar's'. And with her smarts, looks and chutzpah, she had unlimited access to it. But if she was, for many, the 'It' girl of the time, her writing has also proven her to be a substantial documenter of that hedonistic era.

The daughter of an artist mother and violinist father, Babitz attended a school populated by the children of movie stars, noting in her first book, *Eve's Hollywood* (1974), that the local gene pool was geared towards intimidating levels of beauty. Not that she came up short on looks or connections. As she says of herself, 'I looked like Brigitte Bardot and I was Stravinsky's goddaughter.' At twenty, she famously posed for a photo with Marcel Duchamp, playing chess with him while nude. She was one of Ed Ruscha's 'Five 1965 Girlfriends' (1970),

had affairs with some of the most iconic figures of the era and has been fabulously indiscreet about them. Babitz's LA is a gleaming pop-light contrast to the foreboding darkness of Joan Didion's portraits. In her world, the present was everything. The future could wait.

Eve's Hollywood reads like a series of missives about the people, culture and landscape that dominated the writer's youth. It opens with seven pages of acknowledgements listing everyone and everything that inspired her. Then there's a snippet of conversation: '"Where are you from?" "Hollywood." "Born there too?" "Yeah." "…What was it like?" "Different".' It sets the tone of a place that seems so familiar yet remains otherworldly. Each chapter evinces spontaneity and jubilance – the style is conversational but never so lazy as to feel gossipy. And just occasionally there's a hint of acknowledgement that the party can't last. *Slow Days, Fast Company* (1977) emphasizes this, but the party continues. As it does in *Black Swans* (1993), Babitz's last book and her portrait of LA in the 1980s and 90s. But there's a sharper edge to this, a bittersweet acceptance even, that the more 'innocent' early days are gone for good.

J.G. BALLARD (1930–2009)

—— THE SUBURBAN SOOTHSAYER

Childhood wartime experiences moulded the character of a writer who came to dominate a new era in speculative fiction and radical dystopian portraits of contemporary life.

Born and raised among the British ex-pat community in 1930s China, James Graham Ballard and his family were taken captive by Japanese forces and imprisoned in a civilian internment camp until the end of World War II. These experiences, recounted in the writer's semi-autobiographical novel *Empire of the Sun* (1984), informed Ballard's portraits of humanity in tumult or edging towards an environmental doomsday.

Ballard initially studied medicine at Cambridge, but changed to a literature degree with the intention of becoming a writer. While serving in the Royal Air Force in a remote part of Canada, he devoured American sci-fi magazines and wrote his first work of speculative fiction, *Passport to Eternity* (1963). On returning to England, he was regularly featured in *New Worlds* and *Science Fantasy*, but as his style became increasingly experimental it conflicted with those publications' more mainstream tastes. Antithetical to the philosophical and political worldview of much science fiction, he found a more welcoming environment in *Gambit*, which he also edited. Working alongside artists, poets and essayists, Ballard developed a style that was heavily influenced by psychoanalysis, Surrealism and the nascent Pop Art movement.

The conceptual *The Atrocity Exhibition* (1970), a collection of experimental pieces, attracted considerable attention and controversy. It was subject to obscenity charges in the US and its publisher demanded all copies be pulped. Among the stories was 'Crash', which drew a direct line between sex and the automobile, and was embellished upon in one of Ballard's most notorious novels, *Crash* (1973). It was followed by *Concrete Island* (1974) and *High-Rise* (1975), rounding out a trilogy that set up one-day-in-the-future scenarios that tapped into an increasingly depersonalized and concretized world.

The suburbs of southwest London, to which Ballard moved in 1960, were frequently the setting or inspiration for much of the author's subsequent fiction. The themes of his early, now unnervingly prescient environmental novels, such as *The Drowned World* (1962) and *The Drought* (1965), continued in the later works *Hello America* (1981), *The Day of Creation* (1987) and *Rushing to Paradise* (1994). These existed alongside anxious state-of-society surveys *Running Wild* (1988), *Cocaine Nights* (1996), *Super-Cannes* (2000), *Millennium People* (2003) and *Kingdom Come* (2006), which have proven no less prophetic in the portrait of societies obsessed with consumerism and the rise of xenophobic hysteria. His writing earned him the moniker 'the seer of Shepperton'.

DJUNA BARNES (1892–1982)

—— THE AVANT-GARDIST

A writer whose work ran the gamut of style and form, Djuna Barnes is one of the more colourful figures of 20th-century American letters.

Born in Cornwall-on-Hudson, some fifty miles north of New York City, Barnes's father, an unsuccessful musician and artist, was a polygamist who lived with both Barnes's mother and his mistress. Mostly raised by her writer and activist grandmother – a key member of the women's suffrage movement – Barnes was initially educated at home. Although she never confirmed rumours that she was sexually abused as a child, both her autobiographical debut novel *Ryder* (1928), which she described as 'a female *Tom Jones*', and her final play *The Antiphon* (1958) hint at such events taking place.

Barnes had a sporadic period of formal education at the Pratt Institute and the Art Students League of New York between 1912 and 1916, and shortly after became a staff writer at the *Brooklyn Daily Eagle*. Her ability to write with style at great speed, along with her skill as an illustrator, soon found her working at major New York newspapers. Her approach was often unconventional, and interviews were sometimes irreverent. Politics, particularly women's suffrage and gender inequality, was a mainstay of Barnes's journalism, while her desire to experiment further found a home in her fiction. She published short stories in several local newspapers and magazines, produced an offbeat chapbook entitled *The Book of Repulsive Women: 8 Rhythms and 5 Drawings* (1915) and wrote a variety of plays that were produced by the influential Provincetown Players.

Barnes found her spiritual and creative home in Paris, and moved there in 1921. Her fiction collection *A Book* (1923) established her literary credentials and was followed by *Ryder*. She became one of the luminaries of the city's art and literary scene, alongside her lover, the artist Thelma Wood. That relationship, after it ended, formed the basis of Barnes's most influential novel *Nightwood* (1936), a classic of lesbian fiction and the summation of Barnes's interest in modernist writing.

A few years after its publication and following a suicide attempt, she returned to New York. An alcoholic by this time, Barnes moved to Greenwich Village, where she would live out her life, her writing becoming less frequent until she stopped drinking in the early 1950s. Increasingly reclusive, her final work was the raging *The Antiphon*. She frequently received visits from illustrious admirers, but rarely answered their calls. To Carson McCullers, who visited in the late 1950s, she called down from an open window, 'Whoever is ringing this bell, please go the hell away.'

“ ANY DAMN FOOL CAN BEG
UP SOME KIND OF JOB; IT
TAKES A WISE MAN TO MAKE
IT WITHOUT WORKING. ”

POST OFFICE

CHARLES BUKOWSKI (1920-1994)

—— THE DAUPHIN OF THE DISPOSSESSED

A writer whose stories detailed the lives of the dispossessed and poverty-stricken on the fringes of US society.

Unlike Oscar Wilde, Charles Bukowski never looked further from the gutter than a bottle of bourbon. But the short distance from the street to a local bar, via a series of turbulent relationships, banal jobs and measly pay cheques that sustained him, would inspire a body of work that read like missives from the underbelly of America.

Heinrich Karl Bukowski was born in Andernach, in the Rhine Province of what was then the Weimar Republic. He moved with his family to the US in 1923, settling in Los Angeles in 1930. Bukowski claims that the extreme physical and mental abuse his father inflicted on him, along with his terrible acne and bullying at school, found him increasingly withdrawn. These factors, he later noted, helped him understand that cruelty and pain were often undeserved. Early exposure to alcohol allowed him to escape reality, and his experiences eventually found their way into his writing. His first published story, 'Aftermath of a Lengthy Rejection Slip' (1944), plays out like a snapshot from his life. It was published by *Story*, one of dozens of small magazines and publishers that Bukowski aligned himself with, regularly sending poems, short stories, essays and fragments of material. None was more important in the development of his career than Black Sparrow Press. Its owner, John Martin, recognized Bukowski's genius when most US critics failed to. His writing lacked the formal invention or passion of the Beat movement and was a world away from what was regarded as 'serious' literature. But in Europe, it found supporters. And their championing of him finally saw Bukowski embraced by the US literary establishment, albeit posthumously.

It's impossible to look at Bukowski's writing without recognizing the elements of autobiography. His day-to-day employment, most notably his years working for the Los Angeles division of the United States Post Office Department, which informed his first published novel *Post Office* (1971), along with his various personal relationships, all played a significant role in his creative process. The experiences contributed to the authenticity and stark, often deeply unpalatable, honesty of his stories and poems. Reviled by some, he was a literary trailblazer to others. The controversial nature of his work even attracted the attention of the FBI. The government agency kept a file on him for a while, primarily because of his late 1960s newspaper column 'Notes of a Dirty Old Man', detailing the minutiae of his life with alcohol and his many personal and professional mishaps.

MIKHAIL BULGAKOV (1891-1940)

—— THE SUBVERSIVE

Mikhail Afanasyevich Bulgakov never lived to see his most important work of fiction acclaimed as one of the greatest and most subversive novels of the 20th century.

Born in Kiev, then under the control of the Russian Empire, his father, Afanasiy, was a state councillor and assistant professor at Kiev Theological Academy, renowned as an intellectual and translator of religious texts. Bulgakov was a student at First Kiev Gymnasium, where he displayed an interest in literature and the performing arts. Following the death of his father in 1907, Bulgakov's mother Varvara assumed control of his education and exerted a heavy influence over him.

After graduating from the medical faculty at Kiev University, Bulgakov served in World War I as a doctor, sustaining wounds that would trouble him throughout his life. His addiction to painkillers during this period, along with his wartime experience, was recounted in his 1926 story 'Morphine', which became part of his fiction collection *A Country Doctor's Notebook*. It was written throughout the early 1920s and based on his medical experiences in the period dominated by the Russian Revolution. That career came to an abrupt end when, while carrying out his duties as a physician in the Ukrainian People's Army, which was aligned with the ousted Tsarist regime, he contracted typhus. From that point on, he committed to being a writer.

His first collection, *Future Perspectives*, brought together his newspaper writings and was followed by two plays, *Self Defence* and *The Turbin Brothers*. However, it was his 1926 novel *The White Guard* – only published in serial form and as the play *The Days of the Turbins* in his lifetime – that established him. Opening in 1918 and featuring autobiographical elements, it told the story of the Ukrainian War of Independence, but was criticized by the Soviet government for failing to feature a Communist hero. The opprobrium only intensified with the publication of the satires *The Fatal Eggs* (1925) and *The Heart of a Dog* (1926).

Although popular with readers, Bulgakov's critique of Soviet society found him increasingly isolated politically and culturally. It was almost impossible for him to be published, yet a request to emigrate was turned down by Joseph Stalin in 1930. At the same time, his work was developing in richness and complexity. His 1932 play *Molière*, about the French playwright, was staged in 1936 but closed after a week because of its critique of the Communist elite. He followed it with the unfinished autobiographical work *Black Snow: A Theatrical Novel* and his most acclaimed fiction *The Master and Margarita*. A scathing critique of Communist Russia's ruling classes, it was finally published – albeit in a heavily abridged form – in Russia twenty-five years after its author's death.

WILLIAM BURROUGHS (1914-1997)

—— EL HOMBRE INVISIBLE

William Seward Burroughs transformed his drug addiction into a vocation, employing a radical style of writing and editing to create worlds that blur the line between reality and narcotic-augmented fantasy.

Born in St Louis into a wealthy family – his grandfather, whom he was named after, invented the Burroughs Adding Machine – whatever existence Burroughs' middle-class family expected him to have was a far cry from the one he led. His bibliography lists a trove of novels, novellas, short stories, essays, letters, plays, screenplays, collaborations and sketches. There are paintings and documentaries, as well as recordings of his readings and musings. But the life Burroughs lived is as rich, unconventional and experimental as the work he produced.

After graduating from Harvard and with a monthly stipend of $200 from his family, Burroughs was free to explore his interests. He had kept his sexuality hidden during his youth. But his roaming across Europe and Latin America found him becoming surer of his desires, which he explored alongside a drug intake that began with morphine but eventually changed to heroin. He married twice during this period, with his second marriage, to Joan Vollmer, ending in Mexico when Burroughs – a lifelong gun obsessive – shot and killed her. Details of what happened have never been clear – at one point he claimed they were acting out the William Tell myth – but the event had a profound effect upon his life. Magic and elements of the occult were a mainstay of Burroughs' belief system since childhood, and he became convinced that the negative energy, an evil spirit resulting from his wife's shooting, drove him to write.

Burroughs had met Allen Ginsberg and Jack Kerouac after the war, and together they would form the driving force of the Beat movement; the latter collaborated with him on *And the Hippos Were Boiled in*

Their Tanks, which was eventually published in 2008. He published *Junkie* (1953) and completed *Queer*, which was eventually published in 1985. But after encountering Brion Gysin's cut-up technique – an aleatory literary process in which passages are cut up and randomly reordered to change their meaning – and developing with him the fold-in method – taking two pages of print, folding them and joining the folded pages together to create new sentences – Burroughs embarked on a radical new style of writing. It was exemplified by *The Naked Lunch* (1959). Set upon a landscape heavily influenced by Burroughs' time living in Tangiers, his mix of autobiography, wild fantasy and sexually explicit material broke new ground stylistically. It also attracted accusations of obscenity and remains the subject of the last obscenity trial against a work of literature to be prosecuted in the US.

Burroughs spent the next decade living in Paris and London, before moving back to the US for the remainder of his life; first in a basement apartment in Manhattan and then in Lawrence, Kansas. From his role as an icon of the Beat and hippie movement, he was embraced by Warhol's Factory and the subsequent punk scene in New York. Culturally, he remained one of the most influential artists of the late 20th century, a satirist of Western mores and a disquieting prophet of the human condition.

**" .WHEN YOU STOP GROWING
YOU START DYING. "**

JUNKIE

OCTAVIA E. BUTLER   (1947-2006)

—— THE GROUND-BREAKER

In a genre mistakenly believed by some to be the domain of white male writers, Octavia E. Butler's body of work has proven an inspiring and unsettlingly prescient read.

A decade after her death, Butler's tenth novel *Parable of the Sower* (1993) became an unerringly prophetic vision of the US. Unfolding in Los Angeles circa 2024, the city is subject to extreme climactic conditions, pharmaceutical companies are responsible for its citizens' deteriorating mental health, and a new presidential candidate promises jobs aplenty and rolling back federal 'interference' in daily life. The book reflects the acuity of a writer whose career produced a body of work that used observations of the present to foresee potential future realities.

Born in Pasadena, California, Octavia Estelle Butler witnessed the segregation of race that still existed in a progressively integrated society when she accompanied her cleaner mother to work in the homes of white people. A shy child, she sought solace in the local library where she devoured books, particularly science fiction. In her early teens, she began mapping out a world that would eventually form the spine of her Patternist series. After leaving Pasadena City College, she took a series of undemanding jobs so she could write in her spare time, and at one writing workshop she met Harlan Ellison, who read 'Crossover' (1971) – which became Butler's first published story – and encouraged her to continue.

Patternmaster (1976) was the first in a five-volume series that Butler had been developing for two decades. In it, she envisages a world populated by an elite of telepaths linked by a 4,000-year-old immortal African. She followed it with the Xenogenesis trilogy, beginning with *Dawn* (1987), which introduces Lilith, a black human female whose children go on to feature in the subsequent two volumes. Like the Patternist series, the books explored race, gender and sexuality, and became associated with Afrofuturism. Butler also penned two Parable novels and the standalone titles *Kindred* (1979) and *Fledgling* (2005). In each, she challenges representations of race and gender.

In addition to Hugo and Nebula awards, Butler received a lifetime achievement award from the PEN American Center, and in 1995 became the first science fiction writer to receive a MacArthur Fellowship. Her opinion of being one of the few black writers in the genre, like her thoughts on many other areas, was to rail against stereotyping: 'Why aren't there more SF Black writers? There aren't because there aren't. What we don't see, we assume can't be. What a destructive assumption.'

ITALO CALVINO   (1923-1985)

—— THE FABULIST

Italo Calvino celebrated the richness of his country's myths while inventing many of his own, set in both the past and the future.

In his enigmatic *Invisible Cities* (1972), Italo Calvino imagines a conversation between the great emperor Kublai Khan and explorer Marco Polo, the ruler's captive. He staves off a grim fate, Scheherazade-like, by recounting his experiences as a traveller to the world's most fabulous cities, all of which are a variation on his beloved Venice. Through the creation of myths about these fictional, 'invisible' places, Calvino takes the reader on an exploration of culture, language, space and time. Devised within an almost mathematical structure, the novel represents the playfulness of Calvino's work and his fascination with the mechanics of storytelling.

Italo Giovanni Calvino Mameli was born in Cuba. His parents were both Italian botanists. They returned to their homeland when he was just two, and he and his brother lived a fairly privileged youth, oscillating between a florioculture station designed by their parents on the Ligurian coast, and the land owned by his father's family in the country, which became a frequent backdrop to his fiction, such as *The Baron in the Trees* (1957). He grew up despising the far right and

joined a Communist resistance unit in the latter part of World War II. His experiences were recounted in the short story collection *The Crow Comes Last* (1949).

Early fiction, such as *The Path to the Nest of Spiders* (1947) and the trilogy of quasi-autobiographical tales *Into the War* (1954), showed the influence of Neorealism, but his adherence to the left was broken by his disillusionment over the Soviet invasion of Hungary in 1956. The theme of *The Baron in the Trees*, written over just three months during this period, reflected this. But his fiction was already shifting away from realism and towards fantasy, first with his compendium *Italian Folk Tales* (1956) and then his novel *The Nonexistent Knight* (1959). The nature of identity became increasingly important to Calvino, and as his stature grew – allowing him to travel the world and take up residency at various universities – so the ambition of his work expanded. *Cosmicomics* (1965), which first appeared in the magazines *Il Caffè* and *Il Giorno*, built a bridge between science and fiction, with a 'fact' from one inspiring the other. In the heated political environment of 1968, Calvino joined the experimental literary group Oulipo, and its interest in structure and semiotics would inspire the writer's final works.

ALBERT CAMUS (1913–1960)

—— THE ABSURDIST

Albert Camus drew on the inequality he experienced in his youth in Algeria for his philosophically tinged, politically driven work.

Although routinely referred to as an existentialist, Albert Camus disowned the label many times during his life. Instead, he regarded himself as a moralist, drawing inspiration from earlier philosophical thought, from Nietzsche and 17th-century philosophers such as Descartes, back to ancient Greek philosophers, along with events that unfolded during his early life.

He was born in poverty in Mondovi (present-day Dréan), in French Algeria. With a dual passport, he enjoyed the benefits of being a *pied-noir* (literally, 'black foot'), a French national of Algerian descent. A bout of tuberculosis in his late teens impeded his sporting ambitions and would later prevent him from serving in the French army during World War II. He would instead become editor-in-chief of the banned Resistance newspaper *Combat*, which helped establish his reputation.

Camus's opposition to any form of totalitarianism can be traced back to his witnessing the repressive colonial rule in Algeria. He believed that any political or ideological stance was superseded by a belief in moral righteousness. It was a position derided by both Algerians and French at the height of that conflict.

He was an early champion of a unified Europe, a project he ardently supported up to his early death, in a car accident outside Paris in 1960.

Key to Camus's writings are notions of absurdism and revolt. The former is defined by the conflict between human consciousness and an indifferent universe, while with the latter Camus was keen to emphasize resistance to any form of oppression, which saw him break away from supporters of Stalin's brutal regime. His work appeared in cycles, comprising a novel, major work of non-fiction and a play. The first of these cycles saw the publication of *The Outsider* (1942), *The Myth of Sisyphus* (1942), which outlined the author's notion of the absurd, and *Caligula* (1944). The second cycle, which explored the notion of rebellion, included the novel *The Plague* (1947), the book-length essay *The Rebel* (1951) and the plays *The State of Siege* (1948) and *The Just Assassins* (1949). A third cycle, which would include the incomplete memoir *The First Man*, finally published in 1994, was unfinished at the time of Camus's death.

One of the youngest Nobel Prize laureates, Camus's early death may have contributed to his perennial cult appeal. Like Kafka, his writing is consumed as a rite of passage. But his importance as a moral force in contemporary Western thought continues unabated.

" A NOVEL IS NEVER ANYTHING BUT A PHILOSOPHY PUT INTO IMAGES "

ANGELA CARTER (1940-1992)

—— THE MYTH-MAKER

Myths, legends and fairy tales were transformed by Angela Carter into dangerous and taboo-busting explorations of desire, eroticism and the female archetype.

She integrated feminist thought with popular myths and folk tales. They included picaresque journeys that drew on Shakespeare and Gothic literature, and employed a style of writing that sparkled with wonder yet was frequently infused with a sense of dread. In all her work, Carter challenged traditions, most commonly long-held beliefs regarding gender roles, often upturning the way women were represented as submissive or victims. Through Surrealism and fantasy, her novels exposed double standards between the sexes and sought to present alternative outcomes that questioned some people's acceptance of gender imparity in modern society.

Born Angela Olive Stalker in Eastbourne, after a brief stint as a journalist, Carter studied Medieval Literature at Bristol University. Her first novel, *Shadow Dance* (1966), soon followed. It told the story of Honeybuzzard (by which the novel is also known) and the two personas he adopts by day and night. The novel was acclaimed by Anthony Burgess for displaying 'a capacity for looking at the mess of contemporary life without flinching', and has been grouped with Carter's third and fifth novels,

Several Perceptions (1968) and *Love* (1971), referred to as the 'Bristol Trilogy' for their perspective on that city's countercultural scene in the late 1960s. Her receipt of the Somerset Maugham Award during this period allowed her to travel to Japan, where she lived for two years. She continued to travel throughout her life, often as a visiting lecturer at universities.

The Magic Toyshop (1967) was adapted by Carter into a 1987 feature film, as was the earlier *The Company of Wolves* (1984), adapted from her short story collection *The Bloody Chamber* (1979), which was responsible for her commercial breakthrough. These two screenplays highlight Carter's versatility beyond her nine novels. She was a regular columnist and critic, produced nine collections of short stories, three poetry anthologies, several plays for radio and the stage, and translations of fairy tales. She also wrote and narrated the controversial television documentary *The Holy Family Album* (1991), which depicted representations of Christ in Western art.

In 2012, Carter's 1984 novel *Nights at the Circus* was named as the winner of the Best of the James Tait Black Memorial Prize. The author had been dead for two decades, but for her work has continued to grow in importance and popularity.

COLETTE (1873-1954)

—— THE RULE BREAKER

Journalist, actor, mime artist and provocateur, Colette challenged societal norms to live her life as she wanted, while producing a Nobel Prize-winning body of fiction that celebrated the sensuality of the world around us.

Born into a middle-class family in provincial France, Sidonie-Gabrielle Colette's journey into the heart of the Parisian *beau monde*, her marriage to publisher and renowned libertine Henry Gauthier-Villars (aka 'Willy'), his appropriation of her early writings and her eventual disentanglement from his grasp might have latterly become the best-known period of her life – in part because of the films *Becoming Colette* (1991) and *Colette* (2018), which focus on these years – but Colette's whole life was creatively and personally adventurous.

There's no doubt that Willy introduced his younger wife to a very different world to the one she grew up in. He even gave her the idea for the four Claudine books (*Claudine at School*, *Claudine in Paris*, *Claudine Married* and *Claudine and Annie*), published between 1900 and 1903. Colette herself acknowledged his encouragement of her as a writer. But Willy's unwillingness to give her credit for her own work, his retention of the considerable royalties from the book sales, along with his excessive lifestyle, eventually resulted in their separation in 1906 and divorce in 1910. Eventually, Willy publicly acknowledged Colette's authorship of the Claudine series.

Possessing little money following her separation, Colette embarked on a stage career, travelling across the country to perform in music halls. Her experiences influenced her 1910 novel *The Vagabond*, which highlighted the challenges women face in achieving independence in French society. During this period, Colette engaged in a number of lesbian affairs, most notably with Mathilde de Morny, the Marquise de Belbeuf. Their on-stage kiss during a

pantomime in 1907 was reported to have caused a near-riot.

During World War I, Colette focused on journalism. She had married Henry de Jouvenel, the editor of *Le Matin*, and had a daughter with him, but their union ended in 1924 following the disclosure of his infidelity and her affair with her sixteen-year-old stepson. The following year she met Maurice Goudeket, with whom she remained until her death. By that time, her standing on the French literary landscape was unimpeachable. The 1920s and 1930s were her most creatively fruitful period, beginning with the novel *Chéri* (1920), which, like her most famous work from this time, was set during the Belle Époque and often featured elements of her own life. She also wrote more pastoral fiction, such as *My Mother's House* (1922), a rapturous evocation of childhood, as well as the shorter works *The Cat* (1933) and *Duo* (1934), which examined, respectively, female sexuality and jealousy.

During the early part of the German occupation of France, Colette was fearful that her husband, a Jew, would be arrested by the Nazis. She penned two volumes of memoir during this time, which were published in English as *Looking Backwards* (1941/42), before writing what is arguably her most famous novel, *Gigi* (1944). The Nobel committee nominated her for the Prize in Literature in 1948, as she continued to write. Although she lived long enough to see the 1949 French film and 1951 English stage version of *Gigi*, Colette did not survive to witness the Oscar success of the 1958 Hollywood musical adaptation.

MARYSE CONDÉ (1937)

—— THE HISTORIAN

Entering the literary world at forty with a novel deemed so incendiary that it was pulled from publication, Maryse Condé distilled issues of race and colonialism alongside an examination of gender roles.

Born Maryse Boucolon in Pointe-à-Pitre, the largest city of Guadeloupe, Condé has described her childhood as one dominated by shyness. She preferred to read or tell stories to Danielle, the Indian girl her parents had adopted, than spend time on beaches or with children her own age. Her passion for literature was sparked by reading Emily Brontë's *Wuthering Heights*, which became an inspiration for *Windward Heights* (1995), transposing the lovers – and changing Heathcliffe's name to Razyé – to her homeland and employing a language in the novel's original version that Condé stated was 'neither in French nor Creole. . . I write in Maryse Condé'. How language is perceived is central to Condé's work, primarily because of her history – she is the descendant of African slaves transported to the Caribbean.

After graduating from school, Condé attended college in Paris, first at Lycée Fénelon and then the Sorbonne, majoring in English. From 1960, she taught in Guinea, Ghana – from which she was expelled because of her political views – and Senegal, before returning to Paris in 1972 to teach Francophone literature, and eventually, in 1975, gaining a PhD in the comparative study of black stereotypes in Caribbean literature. The journey taken by the protagonist of her first novel *Heremakhonon* (1976) reflects Condé's own, but she has repeatedly stated it is not autobiographical. However, that character's libertine worldview and behaviour provoked outrage and the novel was banned for a time in France.

Condé's work explores historical events in order for her to explore issues of race and gender, such as the use of the Salem witch trials in *I, Tituba: Black Witch of Salem* (1986). The writer's subsequent novel *Segu* (1987) proved to be her international breakthrough, unfolding in what is now Mali and telling the story of the impact of the slave trade, world religions and colonialism upon the members of an African royal family in the 18th and 19th centuries. Two years later, she wrote a sequel, *The Children of Segu* (1989).

Since the mid-1980s, Condé has taught at universities in the US. In addition to writing plays and children's fiction, recent work includes the memoir *Only Tales From The Heart: True Stories From My Childhood* (1998) and *Victoire* (2006), a portrait of her maternal grandmother. In 2001, the French government named her a Commandeur de l'Ordre des Arts et des Lettres, and in 2018 she was awarded the New Academy Prize in Literature, in lieu of the Nobel Prize not being awarded.

JULIO CORTÁZAR   (1914–1984)

—— THE INNOVATOR

His narrative dexterity was cemented by a ground-breaking novel and a coolness distilled by Michelangelo Antonioni and Jean-Luc Godard's adaptations of his short stories.

The Latin American Boom saw a group of relatively young, upcoming novelists from the region gain traction on the world's literary stage. At the vanguard was Gabriel Garcia Márquez of Colombia, Mario Vargas Llosa of Peru, Carlos Fuentes of Mexico and Julio Cortázar of Argentina. Reflecting the shifting political environment of their homelands, these writers embraced innovation and experimentation, drawing on the modernist movement but infusing it with their countries' own social and cultural aesthetic. Key among the early works is *Hopscotch* (1963), the novel that Cortázar is best remembered for.

Born in Belgium during World War I, Cortázar's parents moved around Europe before returning to Argentina in 1919. His father left soon after and he was raised by his mother in the Buenos Aires suburb of Banfield, which was immortalized in several of his stories. After an unmemorable education, Cortázar taught for a while, before publishing a collection of sonnets, *Presencia* (1938), under the pseudonym Julio Denis, which he subsequently disowned. In 1944, he was appointed professor of French literature at the National University of Cuyo in Mendoza, but his opposition to the Peronist government forced him to resign his post, after which he became a translator. He wrote the play *The Kings* (1949), but his stature as a writer would be cemented after he went into self-imposed exile, moving to France in 1951.

While continuing as a translator, mainly working for UNESCO, Cortázar published *Bestiary* (1951), his first collection of short stories. It was followed by two further collections, *End of the Game* (1956) and *The Secret Weapons* (1959). Among these tales, 'Las babas del diablo', which was inspired by a photograph taken by Sergio Larraín, was adapted by Antonioni for his film *Blow-Up* (1966), while 'La autopista del sur' heavily influenced Godard's *Weekend* (1967).

By that time, Cortázar had been feted for his second novel *Hopscotch*. Formally daring, it invited the reader to rearrange various parts of the novel in accordance with a plan prescribed by its author. Its play with time was a mainstay of Cortázar's fiction, along with his ruminations on the notion of artistic perfection. He would publish six novels in total and continued to write essays, short stories, poems and plays. During the final decade of his life, he became a vocal opponent of the radical shift to the right in Latin American politics.

DOUGLAS COUPLAND (1961)

—— THE DIGITAL AGE SAVANT

Douglas Coupland emerged from a desert in the early 1990s, carrying with him an era-defining portrait of a generation.

A renaissance artist of the digital age, Coupland's career spans film-making, design, art curation and sculpture, as well as a sizeable body of writing that encompasses biography, criticism, essays and fiction. He has produced his own line of furniture, designed to encourage a more peaceful and nurturing environment for writers, and in 2018 created a 5,000-litre art installation called 'Vortex', a vast container in which a Japanese fishing vessel floats on a sea of plastic objects pulled out of the Pacific Ocean, highlighting their danger to the environment. But for many, he remains the prescient voice who defined Generation X.

Coupland was born in West Germany, where his father was stationed as a doctor with the Royal Canadian Air Force. The family moved back to Canada in 1965, and after an upbringing described by the author as uneventful, he attended McGill University to study science, but within a year had transferred to an art and design college. He continued his studies in Milan and Japan, after which he took a design job in Tokyo, but a skin condition forced him to return to Canada. Before he left, Coupland sent a postcard to a friend in Vancouver, whose husband read it and offered him a job

writing on the magazine he edited. Originally intended to support him until his design work took off, writing gradually became Coupland's main occupation.

In 1989, Coupland retreated to the Mojave Desert to write what was originally meant to be a handbook for the generation that followed the Baby Boomers, but eventually became *Generation X: Tales for an Accelerated Culture* (1991), a framed narrative that tells the story of a group of twenty-somethings, interspersed with a series of satirical footnotes. Not a huge success initially, word of mouth saw the book gain stature and, against Coupland's own reservations, he became regarded as the voice of a generation. *Shampoo Planet* (1992) came next and focused on 'Global Teens', as he referred to them in his debut, better known now as Generation Y.

It was while writing for the recently founded *Wired* magazine in 1994 that Coupland's attention was drawn to the rapidly expanding tech world of Palo Alto and the rise of information companies. His research resulted in an article and then the epistolary novel *Microserfs* (1995) and, a decade later, *jPod* (2006). Like Coupland's subsequent novels and non-fiction work, along with his activities in other disciplines, they find him at the locus where culture, technology and human lives interact.

" WHEN YOU'RE YOUNG
YOU ALWAYS FEEL THAT LIFE
HASN'T YET BEGUN...BUT THEN
SUDDENLY YOU'RE OLD AND THE
SCHEDULED LIFE DIDN'T ARRIVE **"**

LIFE AFTER GOD

PHILIP K. DICK (1928–1982)

—— THE ALTERNATE REALIST

One of the most celebrated science fiction authors of all time, whose work never attracted widespread popularity in his lifetime, the paranoia that Philip K. Dick experienced was reflected in his hugely influential and unerringly prophetic writing.

Shortly after Philip K. Dick's death from a stroke in 1982, *Blade Runner*, a visionary screen adaptation of his *Do Androids Dream of Electric Sheep?* (1968) opened. It was followed in subsequent years by the adaptations *Total Recall* (1990/2012), *Minority Report* (2002), *A Scanner Darkly* (2006), *The Adjustment Bureau* (2011), and a major television series inspired by his 1962 breakthrough *The Man in the High Castle* (2015–2019). In 2007, the Library of America brought out a volume of Dick's collected works, making him the first science fiction author to be published by the institution. It's an extraordinary turnaround for a writer who experienced limited commercial success in his lifetime, often struggling to survive through his profession, but nevertheless achieving the status of a cult figure in a genre densely populated by them.

Philip Kindred Dick was born prematurely in Chicago. He had a twin sister, but she died six weeks after their birth, an event that Dick claimed marked him for life. Through his studies at university, Dick came to question the nature of reality; that the world we live in may not be real. This notion channelled its way into so much of his writing, along with a deep distrust of institutions and corporate structures, which became the locus of his ire, as represented in shadowy organizations such as the Rosen Association in *Do Androids Dream of Electric Sheep?*, Runciter Associates in *Ubik* (1969) and the corporatized government of 'We Can Remember It for You Wholesale' (1966). At the same time, individual realities were called into doubt, or our perception of the world was questioned. This is evident in Dick's first published story, 'Roog' (1953),

> **"MY MAJOR PREOCCUPATION IS THE QUESTION, 'WHAT IS REALITY?'"**

which he described in a 1978 essay about his work as being about 'a dog who imagined that the garbagemen who came every Friday morning were stealing valuable food which the family had carefully stored away in a safe metal container'. *A Scanner Darkly* (1977) pushed the question of identity to its limit – and drew on Dick's own experiences within the West Coast drug culture – when an undercover police agent pursues a suspect whose excessive drug use stops the cop realizing he is chasing himself.

The Man in the High Castle (1962) won Dick the prestigious Hugo Award in 1963, but his desire for mainstream recognition and success eluded him. By that time, he had been a professional writer for over a decade and often struggled to make ends meet for his family. Having suffered from anxiety since an early age, Dick's mental state was fragile in later life. Various therapy treatments helped little, but they were explored in novels such as *A Scanner Darkly*, the semi-autobiographical *Radio Free Albemuth* (1976), and the acclaimed VALIS trilogy, which became the final works by a troubled man whose brilliance had long been acknowledged by his peers but only attracted wider audiences after his death.

JOAN DIDION (1934)

—— THE CHRONICLER

She trailblazed at the vanguard of New Journalism, captured the darker side of the 1960s counterculture, called out injustice, and was a supremely gifted novelist, screenwriter and memoirist.

The eponymous essay of Joan Didion's 1979 essay collection *The White Album* features one of the great opening lines: 'We tell ourselves stories in order to live', she informs us. But the underlying suggestion is that there can sometimes be a disconnect between what has happened and the meaning, or interpretation, we give it. It's a typically pithy statement by Didion, whose career in fiction and journalism was driven by the search to find her own path in examining the cultural, political and personal.

Born in Sacramento, California, Didion was a shy child, suggesting in the memoir *Where I Was From* (2003) that the nomadic lifestyle her family led, because of her father's job in the Army Air Corps during World War II, contributed to this. She attended the University of California, Berkeley, winning an essay competition in her final year, which earned her an internship at *Vogue* magazine. An acclaimed article guaranteed her a job and she remained there for a decade. All the time, she wrote for other outlets and published her first novel *Run, River* (1963), which she was later critical of, regarding it as falsely nostalgic.

Her friend and fellow writer John Gregory Dunne helped her edit it, and, soon after, they entered into a relationship, marrying in 1964 and adopting a daughter, Quintana Roo, in 1966. The couple would collaborate on a number of screenplays, including *The Panic in Needle Park* (1971), *A Star is Born* (1976), *True Confessions* (1981) and the 1972 adaptation of Didion's second novel *Play It as It Lays* (1970), a bleak portrait of a starlet's life in Hollywood.

Nowhere is the blurring of the lines between Didion's novels and non-fiction work more evident than in *A Book of Common Prayer* (1977), set in the fictional Central American country of 'Boca Grande', and drawing inspiration from her earlier *Salvador* (1983), which looks at US involvement in El Salvador. To separate Didion's accomplishments into different categories draws power away from her whole body of work and the integrity of it. (She was the first journalist to question the validity of the Central Park Five's conviction in the mainstream press.) In recent years, Didion has turned her steely gaze onto herself, with *The Year of Magical Thinking* (2005) and *Blue Nights* (2011), which detail her life in the aftermath of her husband's and daughter's deaths in 2003 and 2005 respectively. The writing is no less detached and all the more powerful for it.

MARGUERITE DURAS (1914-1996)

—— THE LOVER

Novelist, playwright, screenwriter and film director, Marguerite Duras's life was both uncompromising and lived to the full.

Born Marguerite Donnadieu, she took the surname Duras from the village in southwest France from where her father's family originated. Her parents were both teachers and employed at a school near Saigon in what was then French Indochina (now Vietnam) when she was born. Her father was taken ill shortly after his arrival there and returned to France, where he subsequently died. Her mother and two siblings remained in Indochina, but in relative poverty on an isolated plantation. That part of Duras's life would eventually become the inspiration for her 1950 novel and first major success, *The Sea Wall*. This period was also used by the writer for her Prix Goncourt-winning novel *The Lover* (1984), which she revised in 1991 as *The North China Lover* to coincide with the release of Jean-Jacques Annaud's film adaptation.

Aged seventeen, Duras travelled to France to study, initially mathematics but eventually law. Although employed as an administrator by the Vichy government during World War II, she became a member of the Communist Party and joined the French Resistance, working alongside future President of the Republic François Mitterrand, who would become a lifelong friend. At the same time, she published her first novel *Les Impudents* (1943). After *The Sea Wall*, Duras achieved further acclaim with *The Sailor from Gibraltar* (1952) and *Moderato Cantabile* (1958), which were more lyrical and highlighted a gift for heightened, almost poetic dialogue. This was further evinced with her Oscar-nominated screenplay for director Alain Resnais's *Hiroshima Mon Amour* (1959), a rapturous account of memory and forgetting – or forgetfulness – between a French–Japanese couple. It was Duras's first encounter with film as a practitioner, and it would continue with her writing original screenplays and adaptations of her own work, as well as directing fifteen features, including *India Song* (1975), an adaptation of an unproduced play and arguably her best-known work as a film-maker.

Much of Duras's written and film work is experimental in form, edging towards the Nouveau Roman style that became popular in the 1950s, but she never aligned herself directly with any movement. She refused to be pigeonholed, and her later work even appealed to a wider audience. She continued to write into old age, despite a near-death experience when she employed a radical treatment to give up drinking and, following a bout of emphysema in 1988, a six-month coma. She was a controversial figure, divisive and frequently cantankerous, but her resilience in the face of her critics, the challenges in her life and her own mortality was admirable.

RALPH ELLISON (1914-1994)

—— THE VISIBLE WRITER

One book established the reputation of a writer whose novels and essays helped define a generation of black Americans and were infused with the rhythms and passion of the music he loved.

Ralph Waldo Ellison – named after the 19th-century writer – was born in Oklahoma City. He had an ear for music and began learning the cornet at eight. Leaving school at a young age, he worked in a series of menial roles, but was eventually enrolled on a music scholarship at Tuskegee Normal and Industrial Institute (now Tuskegee University), a respected college for black students. The account of his train-hopping journey there would reach the page in the form of his first published story 'Hymie's Bull' in 1937. Expecting a collegiate atmosphere at Tuskegee, Ellison was surprised by the rigidly enforced social strata of the institution and felt like an outsider.

Ellison moved to Harlem in 1936, then the cultural heart of black America. He befriended Langston Hughes and Richard Wright, whose *Native Son* (1940) was to have a significant impact upon African-American writing of the era. Ellison threw himself into this world. Initially drawn to the Left, he wasn't stridently political, yet saw in socialism a movement actively engaged in fighting inequality.

Enlisting as a cook with the US Merchant Marines during World War II, Ellison saw action in the North Atlantic and began to consider writing a novel. When the war was over, and supported by the income of his second wife, Chicago's Negro People's Theater founder Fanny McConnell (he was previously married to the stage actor Rosa Araminta Poindexter from 1938 to 1943), Ellison focused on completing his life's work. *Invisible Man* was published to great acclaim in 1952. An account of an educated black man's search for identity and individuality in modern America, it drew heavily on Ellison's own experiences, from the economic

> **THE ACT OF WRITING REQUIRES A CONSTANT PLUNGING BACK INTO THE SHADOW OF THE PAST WHERE TIME HOVERS GHOSTLIKE.**

disadvantage of his youth, to the negativity he experienced at college and his profound sense of betrayal by political leaders of the Left cosying up to the bourgeoisie during the war years. Hailed as a masterpiece, with a form that echoes the cadences of jazz, it earned Ellison a place at the high table of American literature. It was followed by collections of essays and, after his death, the publication of his second, unfinished novel *Juneteenth* (1999). But *Invisible Man* remains a key work of both American and specifically African-American literature from the 20th century – in 1965, critics chose it as the most important American novel since 1945 – and a novel whose cult appeal has never diminished.

ELENA FERRANTE (1943)

—— THE ANONYMOUS AUTHOR

Among writers keen to shun the spotlight that comes from their success as novelists, Elena Ferrante alone remains as anonymous a figure as she was when her first book was published.

J.D. Salinger wanted privacy, but the more he tried for it the less successful he was at achieving it. Thomas Pynchon, reflecting the nature of his conspiracy-strewn narratives, literally dropped off the radar, only to have a legion of fans search for him. By contrast, Italian writer Elena Ferrante has maintained a cloak of anonymity that has not only added to her enigma, but intensified readers' focus on the autobiographical aspects of her work.

We do not know what Ferrante looks like. We know little of her life. We don't even know if 'Elena Ferrante' is her real name. What we do know, from the scraps that can be gleaned from the odd interview and the collection of letters, interviews, essays and notes that were published as *Fragments* in 2003 (trans. 2016), is that she grew up in Naples, lived abroad for a period, likely had a child or children, and has worked or continues to work as a teacher and translator. On the question of her gender, Ferrante and other female authors have suggested such questions are rooted in sexism and an unwillingness to accept the success of a female novelist. It's a bitter irony, considering the subject of Ferrante's work; she explores with painful clarity the

way patriarchal society subjugates women and the violence that stems from it.

Ferrante achieved immediate success in Italy with the publication of her debut novel *Troubling Love* (1992; trans. 2006). A letter accompanied the manuscript that was sent to her publisher. It read: 'I believe that books, once they are written, have no need of their authors. If they have something to say, they will sooner or later find readers; if not, they won't... I very much love those mysterious volumes, both ancient and modern, that have no definite author but have had and continue to have an intense life of their own. They seem to me a sort of night-time miracle...True miracles are the ones whose makers will never be known... I'll spare you even my presence.'

If Ferrante's success at home increased with the publication of her second novel *The Days of Abandonment* (2002; trans. 2005), her quartet entitled the Neapolitan Novels, tracing the lives and friendship of two girls from childhood through to old age, brought her a wide international readership. The books' focus, the platonic relationship between two women, was explored in frank and moving detail. An expansive *New Yorker* article by literary critic James Wood praised the emotional and intellectual force of Ferrante's writing, drawing a wider audience to her work. As a result, Ferrante stands alongside Banksy and Pynchon as the most famous artists that few people know.

JANET FRAME (1924-2004)

—— THE TROUBLED SOUL

Portraits of isolation and solitude dominated Janet Frame's writing, seen as a reflection of her own life, which was greatly impacted by mental health issues.

Born Nene Janet Paterson Clutha into a working-class family in Dunedin, in the southern part of New Zealand's South Island, Frame's father was a railroad worker, while her mother was an aspiring poet. Frame's youth was spent in poverty and indelibly marked by the severity of her brother George's epilepsy and the deaths just a few years apart of her two sisters by drowning. It was after the second death that Frame was admitted to hospital, suspected of being schizophrenic, and subjected to bouts of electro-convulsive therapy. All the while she devoured books and wrote.

The severity of her psychological state increased in the late 1940s and reached such a point that in 1951 she was scheduled to undergo a lobotomy. At the same time, her first short story collection, *The Lagoon and Other Stories*, was published, and it was only when an announcement was made that she had received the Hubert Church Memorial Award that the procedure was cancelled. This period of her life was recounted in the first part of Frame's autobiographical trilogy, which consisted of *To the Is-Land* (1982), *An Angel at My Table* (1984), and *The Envoy from Mirror City* (1985). They were eventually adapted into the film *An Angel at My Table*

(1990) by Jane Campion, which elevated Frame's profile significantly internationally, although at home she was already recognized as New Zealand's finest writer.

In 1955, Frame was invited by author Frank Sargeson to live on his property. With his encouragement, she eventually published her first novel, *Owls Do Cry* (1957). It blended poetry with prose and eschewed any semblance of a conventional plot structure in its unsettling exploration of the line between sanity and madness. *Faces in the Water* (1961), written while Frame lived in London between 1956 and 1963, was a fictionalized account of her own psychiatric treatment. But even when she wasn't dealing directly with her own condition, Frame presented worlds in states of chaos, ranging from a group of people who find themselves disconnected from society in *The Edge of the Alphabet* (1962); a girl becoming mute following her parents' separation in *Scented Gardens for the Blind* (1963); a dystopian portrait in Darwinism *in extremis* as a society eradicates its weakest members in *Intensive Care* (1970); and *Living in the Maniototo* (1979), which explores the life of a woman with multiple personalities. Frame's extraordinary skill as a writer brought her attention internationally, but she nevertheless embraced the role of literary outsider and lived her life as privately as she could.

JEAN GENET (1910–1986)

—— THE LITERARY OUTLAW

Jean Genet's life and writings challenged societal mores, attracting opprobrium and acclaim in equal measure.

Genet refused to pander to middlebrow tastes. Occasionally shocking and frequently confrontational, his work reflected a life that was lived almost entirely without compromise. The son of a prostitute who put him up for adoption when he was seven months old, Genet was subsequently raised by various foster parents. He ended up in Mettray reformatory, which prompted his infatuation with the criminal life and men, and was recounted in *Miracle of the Rose* (1946). A spell in the Foreign Legion ended with a dishonourable discharge after he was caught in a homosexual act. For most of the 1940s, Genet led a peripatetic existence, committing criminal acts, prostituting himself and serving jail time. The reasoning behind his criminality, he later claimed, was simple: 'I decisively repudiated a world that had repudiated me.' This period became the backdrop to one of his most famous works, *The Thief's Journal* (1949), which cemented his standing as a literary outlaw.

Following the publication of his first novel, *Our Lady of the Flowers* (1942; trans. 1943), and *Miracle of the Rose*, both penned while incarcerated, Genet attracted considerable acclaim. Jean-Paul Sartre and Jean Cocteau, who referred to him as the 'Black Prince of Letters', championed his writing and, when given a life sentence by a judge after his tenth conviction, successfully petitioned the French President to set aside his conviction. Shortly after, he wrote and directed the homo-erotic short film *Un Chant d'Amour* (1950), and wrote poems and plays that attracted the ire of censors and conservatives. His last novel, *Prisoner of Love*, was published posthumously in 1986.

As the 1960s progressed, Genet became more politically active. He was heavily involved in the 1968 protests in France, as well as communicating with and supporting other activist groups around Europe. Internationally, he was seen as a rebel icon. He was invited to attend a lecture tour by the Black Panthers in the early 1970s, and he supported the imprisoned African-American activists Angela Davis and George Jackson. He spent time in Palestinian refugee camps and, closer to home, gave his support to the prison reform group set up by philosopher Michel Foucault and activist Daniel Defert. All of his work highlighted characters who, like himself, had lived on the margins of society. To many, he was the perennial outsider, whose life and career symbolized the opposition to the restrictiveness and repressive homogeneity of traditional conservative society.

MICHEL HOUELLEBECQ (1956)

—— THE CONTROVERSIALIST

Few writers have attracted such ire from the entire political spectrum as Michel Houellebecq, making him one of the most controversial contemporary French writers.

Houellebecq appears to take great pleasure in self-mythologizing. Profiles and interviews paint a portrait of a man who wears his carnality and rebelliousness as a badge of honour. He even played himself in the 2014 feature *The Kidnapping of Michel Houellebecq*, inspired by a time when his silence, caused by problems with his internet connection, prompted the French press to suspect he had been abducted. But beyond his aggrandizing, his fiction has been unerringly prescient in predicting certain events. It has also been accused of being racist, obscene, pornographic, misogynistic and Islamophobic.

Born Michel Thomas on the French Island of Réunion in the Indian Ocean, Houellebecq lived in Algeria with his maternal grandparents for the first five years of his life, before being sent to live with his paternal grandmother in France, later adopting her maiden name. Attending school and college in Paris, he graduated from the Institut National Agronomique Paris-Grignon in 1980. A short-lived marriage prompted a period of despair that was only alleviated by writing poetry, some of which appeared in the publication *La Nouvelle Revue*. While working as a computer administrator for the French government, he wrote *Whatever* (1994), followed by poems and articles in various magazines. Just as his non-fiction writing has often been dogged by controversy (a 1997 issue of the magazine *L'Infini* featured a divisive piece on paedophilia, while a 2019 article in *Harper's Magazine* was entitled 'Donald Trump is a Good President'), Houellebecq's novels are bleak in their worldview.

Two years before the publication of his 1998 breakthrough *Atomised*, Houellebecq told an interviewer, 'It will either destroy

me or make me famous.' The book was a publishing sensation, but criticized for its graphic depiction of sex, sadism and racism. Nevertheless, it won the Prix Novembre and narrowly missed out on the Prix Goncourt, which Houellebecq eventually won for *The Map and the Territory* (2010). Like his acclaimed novella *Lanzarote* (2000), *Platform* (2001) explored the idea of sex tourism. A significant commercial success, the novel was reviled for its criticism of Islam, and Houellebecq was taken to court over the book, though charges were eventually dismissed. However, the depiction of a terrorist attack on a beach in the book was unerringly similar to the attack that took place in Bali a year later. Likewise, *Submission* (2015) imagined a future in which Islamic law prevailed over France and was published the same day as the *Charlie Hebdo* attack. And in January 2019, *Serotonin*, which features a populist, anti-EU uprising by farmers, appeared to foretell the unrest that would unfold on the streets of the French capital just a few months later. If it sparked less outrage than previous novels, it is perhaps only because the world has grown used to Houellebecq. But he still remains one of the most divisive figures in world literature.

ZORA NEALE HURSTON (1891–1960)

—— THE QUEEN OF HARLEM

Anthropologist, novelist, poet and film-maker, Zora Neale Hurston would become one of the most iconic and revered figures of the Harlem Renaissance, the first major movement of cross-discipline arts in African-American culture.

Born in Notasulga, Alabama, when she was three Hurston's family moved to the Florida town of Eatonville, one of the first all-black towns incorporated in the US and a place she frequently used as a setting for her stories. Her happiness there, documented in her essay 'How It Feels To Be Colored Me' (1928), may have accounted for her much-criticized resistance to racial integration in her later years. Although her formal education was minimal, a teacher had given Hurston a few books when she was young and her appetite for reading grew. Her mother died when Hurston was thirteen and she then attempted to finish her schooling before working as a maid.

In 1917, Hurston began studying at Morgan Academy to complete her basic education, and had to lie about her age in order to qualify for free public schooling, before moving to Howard University, a historically black college, a year later. She co-founded the university newspaper *The Hilltop* and published her first short story 'John Redding Goes to Sea' (1921). In 1925, she moved to Harlem, and shortly afterwards another short story, 'Spunk' (1925), was selected for inclusion in the influential *The New Negro* anthology of fiction, essays and poetry. She became close friends with Langston Hughes and, along with Wallace Thurman, formed the 'Niggerati', a group of writers who produced the magazine *Fire!!* and existed at the epicentre of the Harlem Renaissance.

At the same time, Hurston began studying with noted anthropologist Franz Boas at Columbia University. She travelled around the Deep South, collecting folk tales that would be published posthumously as *Every Tongue Got to Confess* (2001). In 1930, she collaborated with Hughes on the play *Mule Bone: A Comedy of Negro Life in Three Acts*, which was unproduced until 1991. Her research continued, resulting in *Mules and Men* (1935), while her experience of the relationship between powerful white men's 'use' of black women for sexual gratification in lumber camps in north Florida inspired her first novel *Jonah's Gourd Vine* (1934). She travelled further afield, to Jamaica and Haiti – and in the 1940s Honduras – for her research into Voodoo practices. At the same time, she published her most acclaimed novel, *Their Eyes Were Watching God* (1937), a startling portrait of the life of an African-American woman. She followed it with two more novels, *Moses, Man of the Mountain* (1939) and *Seraph on the Suwanee* (1948), and published countless articles over the remainder of her life.

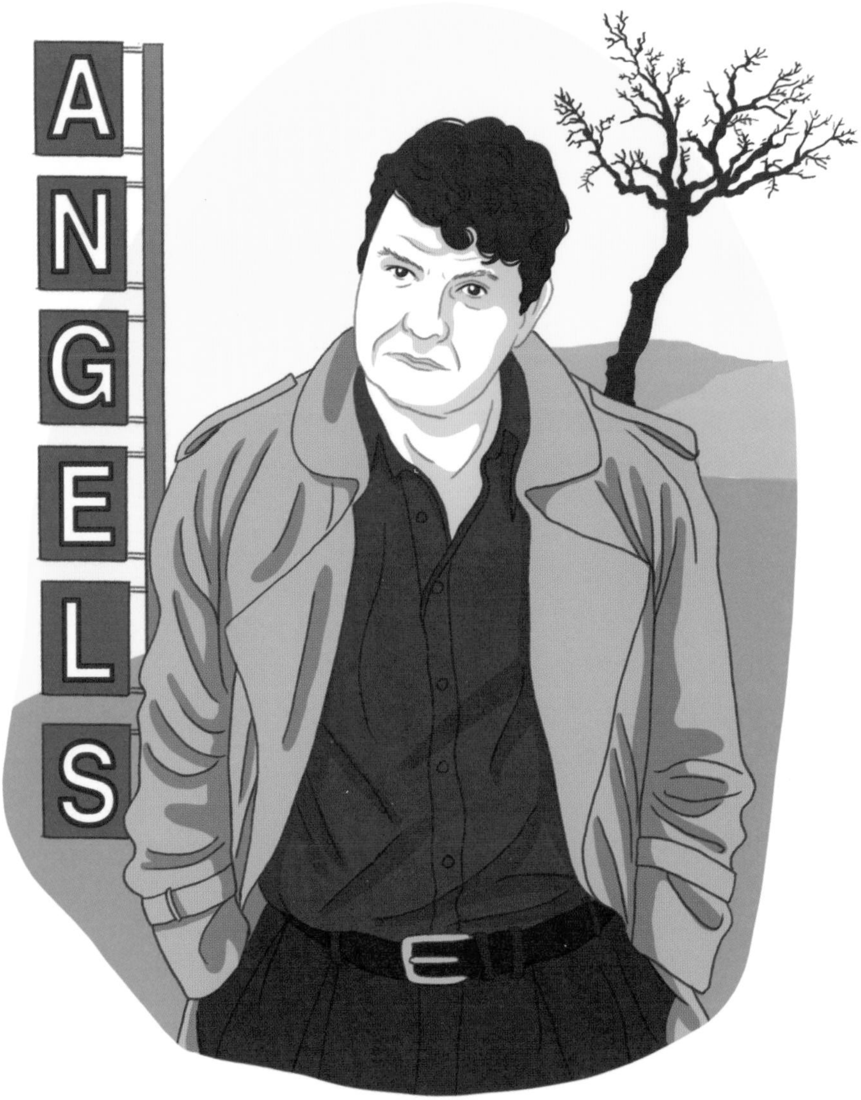
ANGELS

DENIS JOHNSON (1949-2017)

—— THE OUTLIER

Demons drove him and the dispossessed populated his stories, but there was always tenderness and a spirituality in Denis Johnson's portrayal of the fringes of American life.

Johnson was born in West Germany, and as a child his father's work for the State Department required the family to travel the world, finally settling in a suburb of Washington DC. Johnson earned a degree in English from the University of Iowa and completed an MFA at the Iowa Writers' Workshop under the tutelage of Raymond Carver. Johnson had previously published a collection of poetry, *The Man Among the Seals* (1969), and within a few years of graduating received praise for his first novel *Angels* (1983), focusing on outcasts whose lives skirt the criminal world. But he had also become addicted to drugs and alcohol in the 1970s, and it was only after he kicked his habits that he was able to fully focus on his writing. However, his experiences from this period, living among addicts and those on the periphery of 'normal' life, informed his work.

With his brittle, brisk prose, Johnson attracted admirers. Various fellowships and grants sustained him throughout the late 1980s, and each novel published explored a different world. While *Fiskadoro* (1985) contemplated a nuclear apocalypse and *The Stars at Noon* (1986) was ostensibly a thriller set in Nicaragua, *Resuscitation of a Hanged Man* (1991) played out as a Provincetown-set noir. Moral ambiguity tethered itself to characters whose vices and virtues were indeterminate. It was the interlinked stories of *Jesus' Son* (1992) that brought wider attention to Johnson's work. Through one narrator, we drift through the lives and stories of drug addicts and petty cons, with Johnson's ear for dialogue giving his prose a lyricism that could be intoxicating.

Train Dreams was published in *The Paris Review* in 2002 but would become one of his most acclaimed books – nominated for a Pulitzer Prize – when it was published as a standalone novel in 2011. And *Tree of Smoke* (2007), which unfolds in the Manila that Johnson remembered from his youth, earned the writer the National Book Award. He taught from time to time and gave his students three rules for writing, the third of which seemed to reflect his own work practice: 'Write in exile, as if you are never going to get home again, and you have to call back every detail.'

FRANZ KAFKA (1883–1924)

—— THE BUREAUCRAT'S ANTI-HERO

A chronicler of the suffocating repressiveness of bureaucratic institutions, Franz Kafka's literary reputation was only established decades after his death.

For much of his short adult life – he died from tuberculosis aged just forty – Kafka worked in insurance, positions that numbed him with their tedium but allowed time for him to focus on his fictional worlds. His body of work comprises three novels, a collection of short stories, various diary and notebook entries, and letters and essays. (He also left a swathe of reports compiled from his insurance investigations.) But their number pale against the mass of writings he destroyed during his lifetime. Kafka even left instructions with his closest friend, Max Brod, that following his death all his writings, 'in the way of diaries, manuscripts, letters (my own and others'), sketches, and so on, [are] to be burned unread'. Brod decided against this course of action, becoming the safekeeper and champion of Kafka's work.

Franz Kafka was born into a middle-class Jewish family in Prague, then part of the Austro-Hungarian empire. His two younger brothers died young, and his three sisters were to perish in concentration camps during the Holocaust. His father, Hermann Kafka, was a domineering figure, whose behaviour had a significant effect on his son. Kafka's feelings towards his father weave their way through much of his fiction, as well as his attempt at reconciling these feelings in the forty-five-page communication 'Letter to His Father' (1919), which was given by Max Brod to Kafka's mother Julie, who eventually returned it to her son, having never passed it on to its recipient. The short story 'The Judgement', which was also inspired by his father and was written over the course of one night – 22 September 1912 – is regarded as the writer's breakthrough work.

Equally tortured was Kafka's time at the prestigious Altstädter Gymnasium, where students were expected to learn the

> **IF THE BOOK WE ARE READING DOES NOT WAKE US, AS WITH A FIST HAMMERING ON OUR SKULLS, THEN WHY DO WE READ IT?**

classics by rote. This experience, alongside his professional life, unstable relationships, shifting views on his own Jewishness and the prevalence of antisemitism in Prague, as well as the belief by some that he may have suffered from a borderline personality disorder, fed into fiction that imagined paranoid worlds that found characters subject to threats from faceless institutions.

The plight of Josef K. in Kafka's most celebrated novel *The Trial*, written in 1914–1915 but published in 1925, remains the archetype of a Kafka protagonist – trapped in a situation they can barely comprehend and facing charges that are never quite clear – and the worlds he envisaged. K. in *The Castle* (1926), who becomes lost in a bureaucratic labyrinth, suffers a similar fate. Then there's the stranger case of Gregor Samsa in *The Metamorphosis* (1915) – one of the small number of works published in the author's lifetime – who wakes up to find himself transformed into a 'monstrous vermin'. Kafka excelled at exploring the kind of worlds that would become more prevalent in the 20th century, with the rise of totalitarianism and structures of power hidden behind layers of rules, red tape and anonymous bureaucrats.

KEN KESEY (1935-2001)

—— THE MERRY PRANKSTER

Writing a novel that helped define the frustrations of a generation, Ken Kesey became the ringleader of the ultimate 1960s counterculture group.

Born into a farming family in Colorado, who moved to Oregon after World War II, Kesey excelled at wrestling, winning a sports scholarship to the University of Oregon. He switched his interest from play- and screenwriting to literature during the latter part of his degree. He then attended Stanford University's Creative Writing Programme, winning an award for his novel-in-progress 'Zoo', which was never published. He studied alongside future acclaimed writers, such as Larry McMurtry, Wendell Berry, Robert Stone, and soon to be fellow Prankster Ken Babbs, with whom he would form lifelong friendships.

At the same time, in 1959, Kesey agreed to join what would eventually be revealed as a CIA-operated programme that subjected patients to a variety of psychoactive drugs. It would have a profound effect upon his worldview and, alongside his working part-time at a Veterans' Administration Hospital, inspired *One Flew Over the Cuckoo's Nest* (1962). Kesey had previously completed the unpublished 'End of Autumn' (1957), set in the collegiate sporting world, but it was dismissed by its author, who saw his portrait of life on the ward of a psychiatric institute as his true literary debut. Critically acclaimed, *Cuckoo's Nest* was hugely popular and eventually adapted for the stage and an Oscar-winning film.

The novel's commercial success allowed Kesey to move to La Honda, California, where he wrote the successful but more polarizing *Sometimes a Great Notion* (1964). While there, he organized a series of parties known as 'Acid Tests', with invited friends and musicians, including The Grateful Dead, who Kesey would remain the spiritual godfather of. These gatherings would ultimately result in the journey of the Merry Pranksters – a small bunch that included Neal Cassady, the inspiration behind Dean Moriarty in Jack Kerouac's *On the Road* (1957) – across the US, which was seen by many to be the start of the hippie movement in the US and inspired Tom Wolfe's *The Electric Kool-Aid Acid Test* (1968).

Following a brief spell in prison for marijuana possession, and becoming increasingly frustrated by the numbers of hippies visiting him, Kesey moved with his family to Oregon, where he spent the rest of his life. The Pranksters were revived in the mid-1990s and he wrote articles and short stories, but for the remainder of his life Kesey became more private and was happy to let go of the past. His last article, for *Rolling Stone* magazine, was a plea for peace in the world following the terrorist attacks of 11 September 2001.

CHRIS KRAUS (1955)

—— THE AUTO-FICTIONALIST

Admiration for the work of Kathy Acker and a willingness to mine her own experiences and desires have made Chris Kraus a singular and remarkable figure on the map of contemporary literature.

Novelist, film-maker, biographer, critic and publisher, Kraus emerged from the New York art scene in the 1980s. She turned to fiction, or her unique version of it, in the late 1990s with the critically acclaimed and divisive epistolary novel *I Love Dick* (1997), and has subsequently produced a body of work that blurs the lines of the personal, political and cultural.

Born in New York City, Kraus's youth was divided between Connecticut and New Zealand. She graduated from Victoria University of Wellington and worked as a journalist before moving back to New York to study acting and produce films as part of a collective of cross-discipline artists. Her focus was gender stereotypes, which she parodied. Although she continued to make films into the 1990s, including her only feature *Gravity & Grace* (1996) – which, like much of her work, is a study in failure, of people and institutions – Kraus established herself as a respected critic, particularly of the art world, which she often savaged for its patriarchy. Many of her essays for the art magazine *Artext*, which appeared in her column 'Torpor', were collected in *Video*

Green: Los Angeles Art and the Triumph of Nothingness (2004). *Where Art Belongs*, a book-length essay examining sexuality in modern art, was published in 2011, and like all her work, by her own imprint Semiotext(e) / Native Agents.

If *I Love Dick* caused little stir upon publication, its reputation has grown with time, due in no small part to a TV adaptation. Kraus based the story on her own experiences – she even uses her own name for the main character, as she did for her subsequent novel *Aliens and Anorexia* (2000). *I Love Dick* details the stalled potential relationship between Kraus and an academic at a local college, a situation that Kraus's partner also had a hand in engineering. Less a confessional memoir than an auto-fiction, taking actual incidents and presenting them in fiction form, the novel bemused some critics but has since gained stature as a key feminist text of the era. Her subsequent novels also draw on aspects of her personal life. Even her acclaimed biography, *After Kathy Acker* (2017), is complicated by the fact that her former husband was an ex of Acker's. But as the critic Leslie Jamison noted about Kraus, 'Her work isn't an expression of narcissism so much as a preemptive challenge to anyone who might read it that way.'

MILAN KUNDERA (1929)

—— THE SUBVERSIVE

A former Communist Party member who became an advocate of political reform, Milan Kundera was one of the faces of the 1968 Prague Spring.

Born in Brno, in the South Moravian part of what was then Czechoslovakia (now the Czech Republic), Kundera grew up in a middle-class family, the son of an acclaimed pianist and musicologist. His father encouraged him to take up music, but he proved to be more passionate about writing. He initially studied literature, but transferred to film, enrolling at Prague's Academy of Performing Arts at a time when students were beginning to make films satirizing the Communist regime, a movement that eventually coalesced into what would become known as the Czech New Wave. Kundera, for his part, had already struck a sour note with the party. In 1950, he was expelled, along with his friend and fellow writer Jan Trefulka, for activities that were seen to go against the tenets of the organization. He was eventually readmitted in 1956 then expelled for good in 1970, by which time his work had marked him out as a dissident.

Kundera took up a post as a lecturer in world literature following his graduation in 1952. Three years later, he published his first collection of poetry *The Last May* (1955), followed by *Monologues* (1957), which was later banned for being subversive, its exploration of the nature of love excoriated by the authorities for the way that irony and eroticism was brought into play. Over the next decade, Kundera expanded into short stories and playwriting, before publishing his first novel, *The Joke* (1967). Set during the era of Stalin's regime and inspired by his first expulsion from the Communist Party, it attracted international acclaim but faced criticism domestically. His second novel, *Life is Elsewhere* (1969), fared worse and was prevented from being published. This was in no small part due to his role in the 1968 uprising, which saw him campaign for more freedoms alongside Václav Havel. He was fired from his teaching positions and in 1975 was permitted to emigrate to France, taking up citizenship in 1981. It was there that he wrote his most famous novel, *The Unbearable Lightness of Being* (1984), set during the Prague Spring. It adopted a more philosophical tone than the urgency of his earlier work, a style that continued in subsequent publications. He remains in Paris, choosing to live his life away from the glare of the public and media.

66 NO ACT IS OF ITSELF EITHER
GOOD OR BAD. ONLY ITS PLACE
IN THE ORDER OF THINGS
MAKES IT GOOD OR BAD. 99

THE JOKE

URSULA K. LE GUIN (1929-2018)

—— THE SPECULATIVE FUTURIST

Championed for her speculative fiction, Ursula K. Le Guin's prolific output across a wide range of genres evinced her preference for being known as an 'American novelist'.

Ursula Kroeber, the daughter of a noted anthropologist father and acclaimed writer mother, grew up with her two brothers surrounded by books and the study of culture and cultures. Her home received a steady stream of academics, scientists and luminaries (regular guest Robert Oppenheimer was the inspiration behind the physicist Shevek in 1974's *The Dispossessed*), and her parents' projects, most notably working with Ishi, the last remaining member of west Sierra Nevada's Yahi tribe, had a profound impact upon Le Guin. Anthropology would play a significant role in the worlds she subsequently imagined.

Born in Berkeley, California, Le Guin studied Renaissance Literature at Radcliffe College and earned a Master of Arts in French from Columbia University. Accepted on a Fulbright scholarship to study for a PhD in Europe, she met the historian Charles Le Guin on her passage across the Atlantic. They were married and eventually moved to Portland, Oregon, where Le Guin would remain for the rest of her life. Her first published poem 'Folksong from the Montayna Province' (1959) and short story 'An die Musik' (1961), along with five previous novels that had been rejected by publishers, were all set in the fictional land of Orsinia. The failure of these books to attract interest saw Le Guin push her work further into more speculative worlds.

The short story 'April in Paris' (1962) appeared in *Fantastic Science Fiction* and was followed by several other stories, including 'The Dowry of the Angyar' (1964), which introduced the Hainish Cycle. In 1969, Le Guin published *The Left Hand of Darkness*, a key feminist science fiction text and the novel that the literary critic Harold Bloom believed 'more than Tolkien, has

raised fantasy into high literature, for our time'. A year earlier, Le Guin completed the first novel in her Earthsea series, *A Wizard of Earthsea* (1968), fiction aimed at young adults but whose brilliance and imagination outstripped most adult fiction. Some critics have subsequently noted that the Harry Potter series might never have happened had it not been for Le Guin's earlier jaunt into a world of wizarding schools, sorcery and dragons. The books finally saw Le Guin gain a huge following and she became the first female author to win both the Hugo and Nebula Awards for *The Left Hand of Darkness*. She would win both again for her more political novel *The Dispossessed*.

Through her essays and fiction Le Guin championed freedom. She railed against gender inequality and was outspoken in her criticism of capitalism and corporate overreach. When she was awarded a lifetime commendation from the National Book Foundation in 2014, Le Guin was frank about the way 'writers of the imagination' had been received by the literary establishment, and 'who, for the last 50 years, watched the awards go to the so-called realists'. Her belief in the power of speculative writing underpinned her fears for the direction societies were heading: 'We will need writers who can remember freedom – poets, visionaries – the realists of a larger reality.'

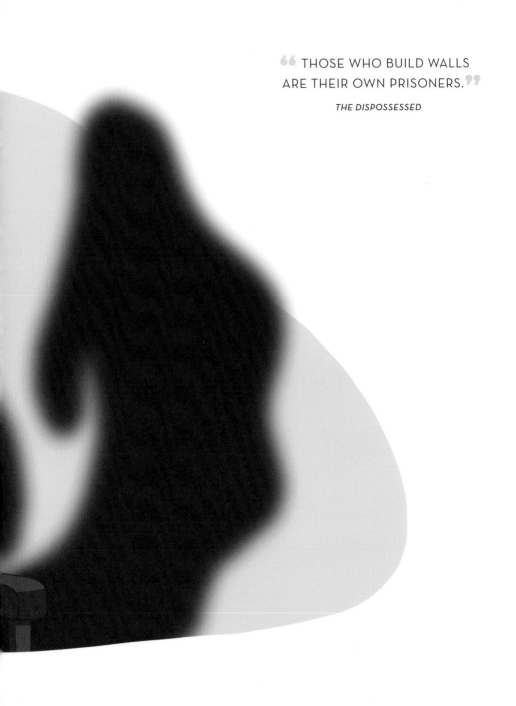

" THOSE WHO BUILD WALLS
ARE THEIR OWN PRISONERS. "

THE DISPOSSESSED

DORIS LESSING   (1919-2013)

—— THE EXPERIMENTER

As her writing blurred the lines between popular and literary fiction, Doris Lessing was uncompromising in her views on gender and political life, and remained provocative to the last.

Born Doris May Tayler in what is now Iran, Lessing's family moved to Zimbabwe (Southern Rhodesia at that time) when she was five. Reading became an escape from an unhappy childhood. She left school at thirteen and soon after was employed as a nursemaid, then a telephone operator, which was when she met her first husband, a civil servant ten years her senior. She gave birth to two children, but was divorced in 1943. She became politicized and joined the Communist Party in Salisbury, married the German lawyer and activist Gottfried Lessing, and gave birth to another child. When that marriage ended in 1949, Lessing moved to London, taking her youngest child with her.

Lessing's marriage experiences and the time spent in southern Africa would inform the first period of her writing career, which began with the publication and overnight success of her first novel *The Grass is Singing* (1950). An account, told in flashback, of the death of a white Rhodesian woman at the hands of a black servant, it was stridently political, a style that Lessing would return to later in her career with *The Good Terrorist* (1985).

At the same time that she produced the ambitious five-volume Children of Violence series (1952–1969), Lessing wrote one of her most celebrated and experimental works, *The Golden Notebook* (1962). A portrait of societal and personal collapse, four 'books' presented aspects of her protagonist Anna Wulf's life, which drew heavily on Lessing's own, while the fifth eponymous 'book' drew together the separate strands and analysed them. It was more internalized than her earlier political work. The critically polarizing novels that followed it, such as *Briefing for a Descent into Hell* (1971), *Memoirs of a Survivor* (1974), and the Canopus in Argos: Archives series (1979–1983), were influenced by Lessing's interest in Sufi mysticism, and ventured into the fantastic and a dystopian future.

Lessing's final novel was the fictional-autobiographical portrait of her parents *Alfred and Emily* (2008), published a year after she received the Nobel Prize in Literature. Two years after her death, the British Secret Service made public a five-volume dossier detailing their surveillance of her Communist activities in the 1940s and 50s, before disengaging with the movement following the Soviet invasion of Hungary. It has only added to Lessing's image of someone unwilling to adhere blindly to the dictates of any institution or doctrine.

CORMAC MCCARTHY (1933)

—— THE WILDEST WESTERNER

Cormac McCarthy transformed the American West into a dark, ambivalent land, chronicling worlds bereft of morality.

It was through his closest brush with the classic Western that Cormac McCarthy finally achieved success. The Border Trilogy, comprising the National Book Award-winner *All the Pretty Horses* (1992), *The Crossing* (1994) and *Cities of the Plain* (1998), spanned Texas and New Mexico as it detailed the lives of two young cowboys from the late 1930s through to the early 1950s. The stories contrast with the bleaker novels that bookend them, but all were written about a terrain that the author knows well.

Born in Providence, Rhode Island, McCarthy attended the University of Tennessee, then spent three years in the US Air Force. His first novel *The Orchard Keeper* (1965) was read by Albert Erskine, who had previously edited William Faulkner, and resulted in the start of a twenty-year professional relationship. *Outer Dark* (1968) was written while McCarthy was spending time travelling in Europe, settling for a while in Ibiza. On his return to the US, he moved to Louisville, Tennessee, where he completed *Child of God* (1973), which was based on the life of an actual serial killer who rampaged through the Appalachians in the 1960s, and was followed by the sprawling, humorous and loosely autobiographical *Suttree* (1979). He

had worked on that novel for almost two decades, mostly through a hand-to-mouth existence that outlasted two marriages.

In 1976, McCarthy moved to El Paso, New Mexico, the setting of his most acclaimed novel, *Blood Meridian* (1985). A savage, revisionist 19th-century Western, it reads like a hallucination drenched in blood, and highlights McCarthy's belief that fiction that matters engages with the most vital elements of our existence: the fight for survival and inevitability of death. Like his subsequent *The Road* (2006), which won the Pulitzer Prize, *Blood Meridian* finds McCarthy at his most pessimistic, embodying in the sadistic Judge Holden the worst tendencies of mankind.

No Country for Old Men (2005) once again found an audience enthralled by McCarthy's vision of the modern West. Originally intended as a screenplay, it was eventually adapted by Joel and Ethan Coen in 2007. The novel's critical and commercial success notwithstanding, what remains remarkable about McCarthy's recent fiction is how his vision remains as true as his earlier work. His world is that of a literary outlier – he has maintained that he would rather spend time in the company of scientists than writers – whose nightmares the reader would hope remain solely in the realm of McCarthy's imagination.

CARSON MCCULLERS (1917-1967)

—— CHRONICLER OF MISFITS

The loneliness of life in the Deep South was conveyed with extraordinary emotional depth and an economy of words in the work of a writer whose own life was defined by debilitating illness and a search for emotional and sexual fulfilment.

Carson McCullers was born Lula Carson Smith in Columbus, Georgia. She initially moved to New York, aged seventeen, with the intention of studying music at Juilliard. Instead, she began to write. Aside from returning home for a few months to recover from a bout of rheumatic fever – the first of many serious illnesses that plagued her – she remained in New York and saw her first short story, the autobiographical 'Wunderkind', published in the December 1936 edition of *Story* magazine. The following year, she married Reeves McCullers, another aspiring writer whose career was put on hold so he could support his wife. They divorced in 1941, remarried in 1945, and Reeves eventually committed suicide, after failing to convince Carson to join him, in their Paris hotel in 1953.

Writing in what is known as the Southern Gothic tradition, McCullers achieved early success with her debut novel *The Heart is a Lonely Hunter* (1940). Its title was taken from a poem by Scotsman William Sharp,

the novel focusing on the struggles in the lives of four inhabitants of a small town in Georgia. Like the rest of her small body of writing, McCullers' strength lay in the way she conveyed the lost spirit of the outsider.

Reflections in a Golden Eye (1941), the novella *The Ballad of the Sad Café* (1943), and *The Member of the Wedding* (1946) bolstered McCullers' success, with the author adapting the last for a successful stage production in 1950. During this period, she enjoyed the friendship of a wide artistic circle. First, in America, she befriended W.H. Auden, Gypsy Rose Lee and Benjamin Britten. But it was after moving to Paris in the aftermath of World War II that she formed a close attachment to Truman Capote and Tennessee Williams. She also expressed an affection for a number of women that is not believed to have been reciprocated.

By the late 1940s, McCullers' health was in a deleterious state. She had suffered two major strokes and even attempted suicide in 1948. But her mind was active and she continued to write. Her last novel, *Clock Without Hands,* was published in 1961, by which time illness had left her incapacitated. She died while writing her unfinished memoir, *Illumination and Night Glare* (1999).

YUKIO MISHIMA (1925-1970)

—— THE NATIONALIST REBEL

A key figure in post-war Japanese culture, Yukio Mishima's prolific career ended by his own hand in a very public demonstration of his beliefs.

At the time of his death, committing ritual suicide following a failed coup, Yukio Mishima, the *nom de plume* of Kimitake Hiraoka, had published thirty-four novels, more than fifty plays, dozens of short story and essay collections, and a libretto, and directed a short feature. A radical nationalist who feared the rise of Communism in his country, yet who annoyed more moderate nationalists for his belief that Emperor Hirohito should have abdicated for his surrendering in World War II, Mishima's reputation is as defined by his life as it is the quality of his work.

He was born into privilege. For much of his early youth he was raised by his grandmother, who refused to allow him to play in sunlight and whose own fears of mortality are believed to have influenced the future writer's obsession with death. Returned to his parents when he was twelve, his father's authoritarianism and strict definition of masculinity saw him destroy anything in Mishima's personal belongings or early writings that hinted at 'feminism'. Such behaviour imbued in Mishima a conflict between his lifelong attachment to militarism and a blurred sexuality that was increasingly evinced in his writing.

Mishima's talents were recognized early. One of his first stories, 'The Forest in Full Bloom' (1944), was published as a limited edition, while his debut novel *Thieves* (1948) attracted enormous acclaim. His subsequent semi-autobiographical novel *Confessions of a Mask* (1949), an account of a young homosexual struggling to mask his identity in contemporary Japanese society – further explored in one of his most famous novels *Forbidden Colors* (1951) – made him a sensation. It also highlighted his stylistic brilliance, drawing on classical Japanese

> **" I WANT TO MAKE A POEM OF MY LIFE. "**

literary styles, but influenced by his love of European literature. He would continue to play with form, through *The Temple of the Golden Pavilion* (1956) and the experimental *Beautiful Star* (1962), to his final burst of creative brilliance, the four novel series The Sea of Fertility (1965–1970).

On 25 November 1970, along with members of Shield Society, his private militia, Mishima entered a military headquarters in Tokyo and took the commandant hostage.

Their aim was to start a military uprising that would support a more traditional idea of a monarchic Japanese society. It failed and Mishima, along with one of his soldiers, committed seppuku or hara-kiri, self-disembowelment followed by beheading. Like his fiction, Mishima's actions were those of an individualist whose ideas often ran counter to popular beliefs, but which defined him as a unique artist.

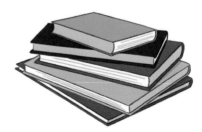

HARUKI MURAKAMI (1949)

—— CHRONICLER OF THE WEIRD

Japan's most internationally beloved modern author has amassed a body of work that plays with genre conventions and exudes an effortless cool.

A best selling novelist, translator, essayist, academic, passionate runner and music enthusiast, Haruki Murakami's fiction evinces the strong influence of Western and Russian literature – attracting occasional criticism at home for not being 'Japanese' enough. He was born in Kyoto and, before turning to writing, owned a coffee house and jazz bar on the outskirts of Tokyo. His first novel *Hear the Wind Sing* (1979), which eventually became part of the Trilogy of the Rat, with *Pinball, 1973* (1980) and *A Wild Sheep Chase* (1982), won a series of local literary prizes. Murakami saw the latter novel as the beginning of his career proper, and he wrote a sequel to it with *Dance, Dance, Dance* (1988). These early works, like his more acclaimed later fiction, explored gender identity, sexuality, loss, the role of technology in society and characters' lives, alienation and, echoing the work of Kafka (who would be referenced directly with the title of Murakami's 2002 novel *Kafka on the Shore*) and Camus, employed absurdism in creating realities that exist outside our own.

Murakami's major breakthrough came with the publication of *Norwegian Wood* (1987), a tale of longing, sexual desire and loss that became a huge success with Japanese audiences and a sensation internationally when a translation was published in 1989. His celebrity reached fever pitch by the end of the 1980s and prompted Murakami to move to Europe and then, in the early 1990s, the US. He took up teaching positions at Princeton and then Tuft Universities, as well as writing one of his most formally daring novels *The Wind-Up Bird Chronicle* (1994–1995).

The Kōbe earthquake and the sarin gas attack carried out by the AUM Shinrikyo in 1995 prompted Murakami's return to Japan, where he has lived ever since. His fiction has continued in its ambition, as evinced by the sprawling three-volume *1Q84* (2009–2010), which takes its title from George Orwell's dystopian novel and explores two parallel versions of the year 1984. Alongside his fiction, he published the factual *Underground* (2000), comprising interviews with those affected by the 1995 gas attack, and the autobiographical *What I Talk About When I Talk About Running* (2008). With the recent publication of *Colorless Tsukuru Tazaki and His Years of Pilgrimage* (2013) and *Killing Commendatore* (2017), Murakami remains a perennial presence on critics' shortlists for the Nobel Prize in Literature.

ANAÏS NIN   (1903-1977)

—— THE EROTICIST

Although widespread critical acclaim only came posthumously, Anaïs Nin wrote for most of her life, fully exploring the boundaries of sexuality.

Born Angela Anaïs Juana Antolina Rosa Edelmira Nin y Culmell to Cuban parents in France, her mother was an acclaimed classically trained singer and her father a pianist and composer. Her parents divorced when she was young and, departing France aged two, she spent her early years in Barcelona and New York City. Leaving high school early, followed by a brief stint as a model, Nin travelled to Cuba where she met and married the banker, artist and soon-to-be-experimental-film-maker Hugh Parker Guiler. They moved to Paris where, while pursuing interests such as flamenco dancing, Nin became more serious about her writing. She had been keeping a journal since her early teens, but her first publication was *D. H. Lawrence: An Unprofessional Study* (1932), notable at the time for being a rare critical appreciation of the author by a woman. Her first novel, *House of Incest* (1936), gave – as its title suggests – strong indications of an affair having taken place between Nin and her father when she was thirty. This period also coincided with her immersion in Surrealism and psychoanalysis, the latter under the tutelage of pioneers in the field, René Allendy and Otto Rank, both

of whom would become her lovers. With World War II approaching, Nin returned to New York, moved in with Rank and for a brief spell became a psychoanalyst.

Having previously immersed herself in the world of erotic writing, like Henry Miller and other struggling writers in the early 1940s, Nin penned erotic stories for money. She continued writing her journals, which played a strong role in the creation of *Cities of the Interior* (1959). The novel's five parts, *Ladders to Fire*, *Children of the Albatross*, *The Four-Chambered Heart*, *A Spy in the House of Love* and *Seduction of the Minotaur*, featured three central female characters who were not only variations on Nin's personality, but also modelled on June Miller, whom Nin was fascinated by and attracted to. There were other characters based on people Nin knew in the book, which contrasted starkly with the style of her final novel *Collages* (1964), which found Nin moving away from a woman's search for identity.

In the 1960s, Nin became a figurehead for the nascent feminist movement. Since her death, her writings have become more popular, particularly with the publication of her unexpurgated journals – a formidable record of observations about her life and of those that orbited around her.

" PASSION GIVES ME MOMENTS OF WHOLENESS. "

SYLVIA PLATH (1932–1963)

——— THE POET

A gifted poet and writer, Sylvia Plath was one of the pioneers of poetic Confessionalism who penned an era-defining novel.

The critic M.L. Rosenthal's term 'confessional poetry' was applied to the poetry of Sylvia Plath, alongside that of Anne Sexton, W.D. Snodgrass, John Berryman and Robert Lowell, whose 1959 collection *Life Studies* was a key landmark for the form. Plath's poems eschewed the reticence, shame and embarrassment of personal revelation, instead embracing it as a way of exploring the psyche and forms of emotional and physical trauma. The apex of these works is *Ariel* (published in 1965), featuring many poems composed in the months leading up to Plath's suicide, revealing a troubled soul that would eventually consume her.

Born in Boston, Massachusetts, to a second-generation Austrian-American mother and German father, Plath began having her poetry published when she was eight. Possessed of a high IQ, her creative impulse extended to a gift for painting. At the age of eleven, she started writing a journal. By the time she attended Smith College, Plath had already produced a voluminous body of work. Her studies were punctuated by a series of academic and literary prizes, which she continued to win after receiving a Fulbright scholarship to study at Cambridge University. It was here, in her first year, that she met and married fellow poet Ted Hughes. They lived together in the US, with Plath teaching at her alma mater, before moving to Boston, where she worked as a receptionist in the psychiatric unit of Massachusetts General Hospital while continuing to write. They returned to the UK in 1959 and their first child was born in 1960. After a miscarriage in early 1961, a second child was born in January 1962.

Plath's problems with depression were present throughout her adult years. She had previously attempted suicide and undergone electroconvulsive therapy, a treatment that was addressed in her work. Although her depression grew worse in her final year, she still continued writing, producing *Ariel* and her autobiographical novel, *The Bell Jar* (1963), upon which her reputation is based. Originally published under the pseudonym Victoria Lucas, *The Bell Jar* tells the story of Esther Greenwood, a young woman interning at a New York magazine over one summer. Detailing the gradual deterioration of Esther's mental state and the oppressiveness of patriarchy in limiting female identity, the *roman à clef* ranks alongside *Catcher in the Rye* as a key rite of passage novel.

THOMAS PYNCHON (1937)

——— THE POST-MODERNIST

His work blurs the line between science and fiction, suggesting the existence of networks of systems that span history and cross cultures, which lie out of sight but affect all our lives.

Drawing on high and low cultural forms, from pulp fiction, b-movies, urban myths and conspiracy theories to linguistic games, cryptography, historical research and a wide array of literary styles, Pynchon's dense, occasionally sprawling novels have polarized critics; some delight in his post-modern games, while others despair at his labyrinthine plotting and tonal shifts. The author himself has rarely commented on his work and, save for an elusive cameo on an episode of *The Simpsons* – in which his character wears a paper bag over his head, he joins J.D. Salinger and Elena Ferrante in famously eschewing the literary spotlight.

Born in Long Island, New York, Thomas Ruggles Pynchon Jr entered Cornell University to study engineering when he was just sixteen, but left in his second year to join the Navy. He later returned to Cornell to study English. His first published story, 'The Small Rain', appeared in 1959 and was followed by 'Entropy' (1960), its title a term that has become key in understanding his work.

After graduating, Pynchon worked as a technical writer for Boeing. At the same time, he was working on his first novel *V.*, which would incorporate elements of his military experience and knowledge of the latest innovations in weapons design. Published in 1963, it was nominated for the National Book Award, which he eventually won for *Gravity's Rainbow* (1973). *The Crying of Lot 49* (1966) was significantly shorter – described by Pynchon to his agent, Candida Donadio, as 'a short story, but with gland trouble' – but it was no less complex. And in its critique of industrial capitalism it highlights the importance of politics in Pynchon's work. During this period, he lived in California and dabbled in the counterculture scene, which would become the backdrop of his most accessible novel, the stoner detective narrative *Inherent Vice* (2009).

Gravity's Rainbow remains Pynchon's defining novel, the *Ulysses* of post-modern literature. It also positions the writer as a forerunner of cyber-punk fiction. Set in the final months of World War II, it is formally brilliant in its knowing play with history, as well as its verbal dexterity – particularly the use of apophasis to hint at events as yet undisclosed to society or to highlight hypocrisy – and dramatic irony. It's a template that he would modulate in exploring the past of *Mason & Dixon* (1997) and *Against the Day* (2006), or the conspiracy-laden present of *Vineland* (1990) and *Bleeding Edge* (2013).

AYN RAND (1905-1982)

—— THE OBJECTIVIST

A divisive figure who sparked a cult of personality and won support from conservatives and libertarians, Ayn Rand was the architect and figurehead of Objectivism.

Elements of Rand's philosophical outlook increasingly filtered into the social landscape of the US during the late 2010s, chiming with the political ascendancy of Donald Trump. A writer who emphasized the self over the collective, deregulation of business over government intervention, and the importance of rationality through her two most famous fictional heroes, Howard Roark and John Galt, Rand embraced the role of iconoclast with abandon.

Born Alisa Zinovyevna Rosenbaum in St Petersburg, Russia, Rand excelled at school but found the teachings prosaic. Claiming to have started creative writing – both screenplays and novels – before the age of ten, she also read philosophy at an early age, embracing Aristotle and disdaining Plato. The Russian Revolution disrupted her studies and her family moved to the Crimea. In 1925, Rand travelled to the US to visit relatives. After a short stay in Chicago, she moved to Hollywood, was employed as an extra by Cecil B. DeMille and, while on the set of his *King of Kings* (1927), met and married the actor Frank O'Connor.

Rand's first major success was the courtroom drama *Night of January 16th* (1934), initially as a film and then a moderately successful Broadway play. It was followed by *We the Living* (1936), a semi-autobiographical account of the author's time in Soviet Russia, depicting the conflict between the individual and collective state. Like the subsequent *Anthem* (1938) – a dystopian fiction set in a society where the word 'I' has been completely replaced by 'we' – Rand's early works would sell in their millions once her fame and cult appeal had been established.

The Fountainhead (1943) set out Rand's worldview and made her a bestselling

> **WHAT IS GREATNESS? I WILL ANSWER: IT IS THE CAPACITY TO LIVE BY THE THREE FUNDAMENTAL VALUES OF JOHN GALT: REASON, PURPOSE, SELF-ESTEEM.**

author. It tells the story of architect Howard Roark, whose singular vision of the built world eschewed the notion of collective thinking that eventually saw him embrace terrorism over compromise. He was the perfect Rand hero, at least until he was replaced by John Galt, the protagonist of Rand's most famous work *Atlas Shrugged* (1957). If Roark saw the world as one he must conquer at any cost, Galt all but gave up on it, choosing instead to create a new one populated by rationalist individuals – artists, scientists, businesspeople and thinkers unencumbered by 'anachronistic' ideas – best suited to an independent free economy.

Rand built up a collection of followers, including the future chair of the Federal Reserve Alan Greenspan, and Nathaniel Branden, who became Rand's lover and for over a decade the gatekeeper of her ideas and estate. Galt's many monologues in *Atlas Shrugged* crystallized Rand's worldview. But like fellow mid-century ideologist L. Ron Hubbard, Rand eventually turned to non-fiction to embellish her ideas.

Atlas Shrugged was Rand's last novel. Instead, she aggressively promoted Objectivism, emphasizing the importance of rational egoism – that individual rights trump all other considerations – and *laissez-faire* capitalism. Her philosophy continues to be treated with disdain by many critics and academics, but her fiction remains widely read.

PAULINE RÉAGE (1907–1998)

—— THE SADO-MASOCHIST AUTHOR

Her infamous novel was published under the pseudonym Pauline Réage, with her true name finally revealed four decades after the literary world first asked, 'Who wrote the *Story of O*?'

In a 1994 article for *The New Yorker*, John de St Jorre told the story behind the 20th-century's most infamous erotic novel. After years of speculation that a man might have penned it, de St Jorre revealed that Pauline Réage was Dominique Aury, a journalist, editor and member of the French literary establishment. To add further mystery to the mix, even the name Dominique Aury was made up; after her death, the author's real name was revealed as Anne Desclos. Born in Brittany, she was raised by her paternal grandmother. An avid reader, she earned a diploma to teach English, but instead became a journalist and translator before eventually entering the publishing world in 1950 with a position at Gallimard, the esteemed Parisian publishing house.

During the war, Desclos had contributed to the clandestine newspaper *Les Lettres Françaises*, which was edited and published by the legendary literary figure Jean Paulhan. Twenty years her senior, he helped Desclos with her book on early French religious poetry. They fell in love and entered into an affair that would last for decades. A renowned womanizer, Paulhan refused to end his marriage for Desclos, and in the 1950s she began to worry that their relationship might end. Their combined intellect the driving force of their relationship, Desclos chose to seduce Paulhan with words and embarked on writing *Story of O* (1954). The novel's dispassionate retelling of a sadomasochistic relationship stunned Paulhan, and he insisted that it be published. Desclos agreed, but only if she could remain anonymous.

The resulting book was a critical success, but when it received a minor literary award in 1955, it attracted the attention of the French authorities. They interviewed the book's publishers, Paulhan and eventually Desclos – how they came to know she was the author remains a mystery – to ascertain whether they should be prosecuted for obscenity. No action was taken. Further controversy arose with the book's US publication, particularly from feminists who objected to the novel's submissive female protagonist. However, it went on to become the most-read English translation of a French book during the late 1960s.

Desclos continued to work for Gallimard into her eighties. She never wrote another novel, but *Story of O* remains a defining work of 20th-century erotic fiction and its influence can be found in the writings of Catherine Millet, Jane Juska and 'Melissa P'.

JEAN RHYS (1890–1979)

—— THE OUTSIDER

A turbulent youth and peripatetic lifestyle led to stories of outsiders, eventually resulting in a piercing prequel to an English literary classic.

Jean Rhys was born Ella Gwendolyn Rees Williams in Dominica, a British Commonwealth island in the West Indies. Her father was a Welsh doctor and mother a Dominican Creole of Scots blood. A testy relationship with her mother saw Rhys sent to live with her aunt in England, but she found life there difficult. She was mocked for the apparent strangeness of her accent, both at the boarding school she attended in Cambridge and at RADA, where her tutors found her voice impossible to work with and advised at the end of her second term that she should leave. This sense of exclusion would give Rhys's writing a unique perspective.

Following the death of her father, Rhys lived a hedonistic lifestyle, which included an affair with a wealthy banker, whose financial contributions supplemented her various jobs, from working in a soldiers' canteen during World War I to being an artist's model. As a writer, she first developed *Voyage in the Dark*, which was eventually published in 1934 and became the third part of a series that included *Quartet* (1928), *After Leaving Mr. Mackenzie* (1931) and *Good Morning,*

Midnight (1939). Heavily autobiographical and bleak in their portrayal of women in the modern world, they were critically acclaimed but failed to ignite readers' interest.

Although she was married three times, the relationships in Rhys's life that appeared to hold greater sway were creative. The writer Ford Madox Ford met Rhys in Paris in the early 1920s. He both encouraged and championed her writing, best represented at that time by the collection *The Left Bank and Other Stories* (1927), advised her change of name to Jean Rhys, and for a while was her lover. Decades later, the actor, writer and painter Selma Vaz Dias sought out Rhys after she had faded into obscurity. Her championing of Rhys's work sparked a creative outpouring that resulted in Rhys's most popular and critically acclaimed novel *Wide Sargasso Sea* (1966). A passionate, feminist, anti-colonial response to Charlotte Brontë's *Jane Eyre* (1847), it told the story of the 'madwoman' in Mr Rochester's attic, the Creole heiress Antoinette Cosway, previously known as Bertha Mason. It was the book that cemented Rhys's literary reputation and attained a cult following. However, for Rhys the hardship she had experienced as a writer led her to the conclusion that 'If I could choose, I would rather be happy than write.'

JUAN RULFO (1917–1986)

—— THE TRAILBLAZER

If his gift as a photographer lay in presenting to the world a unique and singular portrait of his beloved Mexico, Juan Rulfo's influence as a writer stretched far beyond the borders of his homeland.

Rulfo's writing was sparse and his body of work slim, but it offered up stark images of extraordinary beauty, emboldened by the photographs he took as he travelled the length and breadth of Mexico. He was born in San Gabriel, a small town in central-western Mexico. Following the death of his parents while he was still young, Rulfo lived with his grandmother in Guadalajara. The family had once been wealthy landowners, but suffered financial ruin during the Mexican Revolution (1910–1920) and subsequent Cristero Rebellion (1926–1929), which saw more traditional elites fighting President Plutarco Elías Calles's progressive laws that sought to limit the power of the Catholic Church. Nevertheless, Rulfo was sent to a private school.

Unsuccessful in his attempt to study law, Rulfo instead became an administrator at the Universidad Nacional Autónoma de México, where he started writing and in 1944 co-founded the literary journal *Pan*. Taking a job as an immigration agent, which required him to travel the country, as did subsequent work as a travelling salesman, Rulfo took up photography, producing extraordinary portraits of the landscape and the peasants who worked on it. His keen eye observed nuances that would become essential to the passages in his writing that described these worlds.

A fellowship from Centro Mexicano de Escritores in the early 1950s allowed Rulfo to concentrate on his writing: 1953 saw the publication of *El Llano en llamas*, whose short stories focused on the period around the Cristero Rebellion. The collection was followed by *Pedro Páramo* (1955), in which a man returns to his home town only to find it occupied by ghosts. Rulfo adopted a variety of styles in the work, which was greatly inspired by William Faulkner and would have a seismic impact on writing in Latin America. So much so that, in his obituary of Rulfo for *The New Yorker*, the Argentinian writer Ariel Dorfman wondered why the author's death passed with little mention internationally. Perhaps it was that his output was so slim. After all, following the publication of *Pedro Páramo*, Rulfo returned to a quiet life, becoming an editor at the National Institute of Indigenous People. But for Dorfman, as well as other writers who admire Rulfo's work, such as Gabriel García Márquez, Mario Vargas Llosa and Rosario Castellanos, 'Rulfo changed the course of Latin American fiction'.

FRANÇOISE SAGAN   (1935-2004)

—— THE BOURGEOIS REBEL

The prolific author of twenty novels, nine plays, two biographies, innumerable essays and three volumes of short stories was defined by the popularity and scandal of her slim, era-defining debut.

The decision to meet the self-imposed challenge of completing a novel over the course of a few months transformed Françoise Sagan's life. The resulting book was just 30,000 words in length, but its tale of seventeen-year-old Cécile holidaying in the south of France with her roué of a father became a publishing sensation – a cause célèbre that catapulted its author into the literary and celebrity stratosphere.

Sagan was born Françoise Quoirez in Cajarc, in the southwest of France. Shortly after World War II she moved with her family to Paris. Expulsion from two schools for bad behaviour notwithstanding, she was admitted to the Sorbonne, but left before graduating. A voracious reader, she expressed passion for the works of Stendhal, Gide and Proust. It was the character of Princesse de Sagan in Proust's *In Search of Lost Time* (1913–1927) that inspired Sagan's professional name, which she adopted after the publisher who had received the manuscript of *Bonjour Tristesse* (1954) responded with enthusiasm for it.

Within weeks of publication, Sagan had become a household name. Acknowledging the classical style – a writer for *The New Yorker* waxed lyrically that the book could have been 'written on glass, in the simple, permanent, eighteenth-century classic French vocabulary' – and boldly amoral tone, critics showered Sagan with praise. She was hailed as the new Colette and awarded the Prix des Critiques. More conservative tastes decried the immorality of Cécile, concerned that it would present to the world the wrong image of young French women. But that same youth saw in the novel, as others would later with Sylvia Plath's *The Bell Jar* (1963), a new voice that spoke for them.

Sagan enjoyed the spotlight and lived the life of a bon vivant, but continued to write. Her subsequent novels *A Certain Smile* (1956), *Those Without Shadows* (1957) and *Aimez-vous Brahms?* (1959) cemented her critical standing, but all of her work was overshadowed by her dazzling debut. A growing addiction to various drugs eventually cost Sagan her health. But she continued to write, even penning her own obituary for the *Dictionary of Authors*: 'Appeared in 1954 with a slender novel, *Bonjour Tristesse*, which created a scandal worldwide. Her death, after a life and a body of work that were equally pleasant and botched, was a scandal only for herself.'

J.D. SALINGER (1919–2010)

—— THE LITERARY HERMIT

His slim debut novel, examining teen alienation, followed by a lifetime spent shunning the world's attention, made J.D. Salinger a legend of 20th-century fiction.

If there's an archetype for the literary recluse, Salinger has come to embody it. The attention he received for *The Catcher in the Rye* (1951) aroused such consternation in him that two years after its publication he moved to a compound in rural New Hampshire. He continued to write: *Nine Stories* (1953) was a collection of short fiction, which had mostly been published in *The New Yorker*, while *Franny and Zooey* (1961), published in the same magazine in 1955 and 1957, comprised a short story and novella. The tales of two younger siblings of the Glass family, who were a dominant fictional presence throughout Salinger's work (they appear in eight of the author's stories between 'A Perfect Day for Bananafish' in 1948 and 'Hapworth 16, 1924', the last story he wrote, in 1965), they contrasted the busy outer and emptier inner lives of their protagonists. The stories also revealed Salinger's increasing fascination with Eastern religious philosophy.

Two other stories featured in the pages of *The New Yorker* made up the final collection of writing published in Salinger's lifetime: *Raise High the Roof Beam, Carpenters and Seymour: An Introduction* (1963). Both centred on Buddy Glass and extended the writer's integration of Zen Buddhist concepts into his work. A triptych of stories written in the 1940s was published as *Three Early Stories* in 2014.

Born into a Jewish family of Lithuanian heritage in Manhattan, New York, Jerome David Salinger began writing early. He completed a creative writing course at Columbia University and in 1940 saw his short story 'The Young Folks' published. After working on a cruise ship in 1941, he was drafted into the US Army. He partook in the D-day landings on Utah Beach and witnessed the horror of the concentration camps.

After a brief hospitalization towards the end of the war, he saw his short story 'I'm Crazy' (1945) published in *Collier*'s. A story he submitted to *The New Yorker* in 1941, 'Slight Rebellion off Madison', appeared in 1946. Its delay was caused by sensitivities over US entry into World War II. It's protagonist was Holden Caulfield and the story was a dry run for what would eventually become *The Catcher in the Rye*. Debate over the importance of Salinger's novel continues, but its portrait of a sixteen-year-old preparatory school expellee, told in the first person by an unreliable narrator, has held readers rapt for seven decades. Adding to the book's – and Salinger's – enigma is the notoriety of it being linked to Robert John Bardo's murder of Rebecca Schaeffer, Mark David Chapman's fatal shooting of John Lennon, and John Hinckley Jr's attempt to assassinate President Ronald Reagan.

BORIS & ARKADY STRUGATSKY   (1933–2012; 1925–1991)

—— THE SPECULATIVE SATIRISTS

Within the densely populated landscape of Russian speculative fiction, the Strugatsky brothers occupy a singular place.

Answers to mysteries of the universe are far less important than the questions that surround them in the fiction of Boris and Arkady Strugatsky. Even a seemingly straightforward whodunit like *The Dead Mountaineer's Inn* (1970) finds the titular business owner opining to a visiting police detective, 'Haven't you ever noticed how much more interesting the unknown is than the known?' Like so much of their work, that novel begins in a world determined by rules – whether imposed by humans or nature – that gradually ebb away or deteriorate, replaced by a chaos that reflects the author's acceptance of the randomness of life, but also allows for the social critique that became a mainstay of their writing.

The brothers were born eight years apart, Arkady in Batumi, in what is now Georgia, and Boris in Leningrad, shortly after

the family moved there. Arkady escaped the German siege of the city with his father in 1942, but only he survived. He was drafted into the Soviet Army for the remainder of the war, staying on afterwards to train as an interpreter of Japanese and English, before becoming an editor and writer. Boris remained with his mother in Leningrad. After high school, he studied astronomy at university, becoming acclaimed in his field – which provided rich material for the 1965 satire of scientific research institutes, *Monday Begins on Saturday* – before turning to writing in the mid-1960s.

Their first publication was the novella *From Beyond* (1958). *Noon: 22nd Century* (1961), a collection of short stories presented as a novel, created the Noon universe, within which a significant body of their work is set (ten novels between 1962 and 1985). It includes *Hard to Be a God* (1964), an account of a future scientist visiting an alien planet also inhabited by homo sapiens, whose progress has been wilfully stunted in the Middle Ages. In its criticism of a world destroyed by the power of an elite, it was one of the books that saw the brothers accused of being dissidents.

Roadside Picnic (1972) unfolds in the aftermath of a global happening – contact with an alien lifeform. It presents a perfect metaphor for mankind's indifference to the world and its inhabitants. The brothers' most famous work, mainly because of Andrei Tarkovsky's acclaimed film *Stalker* (1979), which they wrote the screenplay for, it best displays the humour, intellectual gravity and imaginative richness of the Strugatskys' intricately conceived worlds.

JIM THOMPSON   (1906–1977)

—— THE CRIME WRITER'S CRIME WRITER

He plumbed the darkest depths of humanity, drawing out of his creative well unsparing portraits of the human condition.

The rawness of Jim Thompson's writing belies his skill as a storyteller, employing unreliable narrators and shifting perspectives that often disorientate, to convey the bleakness of his worlds. He may not have achieved great success in his lifetime, but he is now ranked alongside Chandler, Hammett, Leonard and Ellroy. Thompson was described as a 'dime store Dostoevsky' by US poet and editor Geoffrey O'Brien, and 'the most nihilistic writer ever produced in America' by fellow crime writer Donald Westlake, who penned the script for the acclaimed 1990 adaptation of *The Grifters* (1963), and his life was often as event-filled and tumultuous as the stories he told.

Born in Oklahoma during the Long Depression, Thompson's father was a county sheriff, forced out of office because of corruption allegations. Intelligent but too disruptive to fit into the education system, Thompson started writing young, but wasn't published until he was thirty-six. By that time he had had a variety of jobs – not all legal, become an alcoholic and experienced a few brushes with the law. One encounter, recounted in his memoir *Bad Boy* (1953),

described how a police officer hinted that he could kill with impunity if he chose. He would become the basis of Thompson's most memorable character, the psychopathic deputy sheriff Lou Ford in *The Killer Inside Me* (1952). Lou might be extreme, but he represents the kind of protagonist Thompson wrote about with such conviction – loners, anti-social deviants, and cold-hearted killers and cons. Stanley Kubrick, who worked with Thompson on the screenplays for *The Killing* (1956), *Paths of Glory* (1957) and the unproduced *Lunatic at Large*, described *The Killer Inside Me* as 'probably the most chilling and believable first person account of a criminally warped mind that I have encountered'.

That novel began three years of intense writing, resulting in thirteen books, including his 1953 memoir, as well as *Savage Night* (1953), *A Hell of a Woman* (1954), which highlighted his skill at playing with form, and *After Dark, My Sweet* (1955). His books brought in some income, which was bolstered by film writing and journalism. Although Thompson's output gradually declined, along with his health – the result of decades of alcoholism and hard living – *The Getaway* (1958), *The Grifters* and *Pop. 1280* (1964), arguably his last great novel, displayed the lean ruthlessness of his style.

J.R.R. TOLKIEN (1892–1973)

—— THE FANTASIST

To many readers of fantasy fiction, who consume the tales of vast imagined worlds populated by monstrous creatures, there is one writer to rule them all.

In his review of Episode III of George Lucas's Star Wars saga, *Revenge of the Sith* (2005), the critic Anthony Lane questioned the effectiveness of the writer-director's skill with character names, suggesting 'the resonance of those names is a fairly accurate guide to the mettle of the imagination in question. Tolkien, earthed in Old English, had a head start that led him straight to the flinty perfection of Mordor and Orc.' Certainly, Tolkien's academic career added richness to his detailed portrait of Middle Earth. But beyond his love of language, the writer's first-hand experience of the horrors of battle and the furnace of war arguably gave his most famous creations such visceral, often terrifying power.

John Ronald Reuel Tolkien was born in Bloemfontein, Orange Free State, in what is now South Africa. When he was four, his mother took the family on an extended visit to Britain, but while away his father died of rheumatic fever, so they stayed and set up home in Birmingham. He was an early learner and a fast reader, picking up on languages and creating his own, 'Nevbosh', as a child. His mother died when he was twelve, after which he attended King Edward's School in Birmingham and university at Exeter College, Oxford. He delayed entering the army at the outbreak of World War I so that he could complete his studies. But when he did join up, he found himself in the hellish trenches of the Somme, and only ill health kept him from the battle that killed many of his friends.

As an academic, Tolkien exuded a passion for Old and Middle English, which he taught at Leeds University and then Oxford. He presented an influential paper on *Beowulf*, a decade after he had translated the text. But it was in private that his most famous work began to take shape. A compendium, or 'legendarium', now known as *The Silmarillion* (1977), outlined the world that would first appear in *The Hobbit* (1937), which emerged from a series of tales he created to entertain his children. The darker, more expansive *The Lord of the Rings* (1954–1955) followed. Tolkien continued to write, with many of his works published since his death, but it is for his two towering feats of imagination that Tolkien is admired throughout this world.

KURT VONNEGUT (1922–2007)

—— THE SATIRIST

A tumultuous event may have informed his breakthrough novel, but all of Kurt Vonnegut's work was possessed of an idiosyncratic and often startling worldview.

Descended from German immigrants, Vonnegut was born in Indianapolis and raised in a middle-class household that was affected by the Great Depression, eventually leading to his mother's suicide. The youngest of three children, he would later claim that it was through his African-American housekeeper that he learned the values that would forge the moral compass of his work. Despite being more interested in the arts, Vonnegut followed his father's instruction and studied biochemistry at Cornell University. However, academic life was interrupted by the bombing of Pearl Harbor and he enlisted in the army. It was during the Battle of the Bulge that he was captured and sent to Dresden, a city of no strategic value and which was never seen as a likely target for the Allies. Nevertheless, it was bombed on 13 February 1945. Vonnegut survived the firestorm by spending his days in a sub-level meat locker.

On returning to the US, Vonnegut married his childhood sweetheart, Jane Marie Cox, enrolled at Chicago University to study anthropology, but never completed the course, and began writing for newspapers. He spent a few years working as a publicist for General Electric (GE), but following the publication of his story 'Report on the Barnhouse Effect' (1950), along with a few other short stories, in *Collier's*, where he was coached by its fiction editor Knox Burger, Vonnegut left GE, moved to Cape Cod and focused on his writing.

His first novel, *Player Piano* (1952), set out the style of fiction he became best known for: satire that sometimes drew on science fiction tropes, shot through with a wry humour and, at times, a sense of moral outrage at the inhumanity of people and the systems they create to run the world. Like its successors *The Sirens of Titan* (1959) and *Mother Night* (1961) – the author's first attempt to grapple with World War II – the novels were critically acclaimed but failed commercially. *Cat's Cradle* (1963) and *God Bless You, Mr. Rosewater* (1965) witnessed a development in Vonnegut's style. But it was the perfectly timed anti-war stance of *Slaughterhouse-Five* (1969), recounting the Dresden bombing, that brought Vonnegut success and fame. Deeply distrustful of mainstream politics and an avowed atheist – which was a key factor in the end of his first marriage, at his best Vonnegut identified the fallibility of humanity, yet his work always evinced a faith in the individual.

IRVINE WELSH (1958)

—— THE VERNACULARIST

A working-class upbringing and a turbulent youth provided the inspiration for stories of addition, disaffection and criminality.

In a 2018 interview celebrating the twenty-fifth anniversary of the publication of his debut novel, Welsh said with a note of surprise, 'I thought *Trainspotting* would be a cult book, but not generation-defining.' How much of its iconic status is due to Danny Boyle's equally successful 1996 film adaptation is open to debate. But in its portrait of a group of disaffected Scottish dropouts and its use of vernacular language, *Trainspotting* was regarded as the rebellious upstart of contemporary British fiction.

Welsh was born in Leith, the port area of Edinburgh. Leaving school at sixteen, he took a series of jobs, including a TV repairman, before moving to London and becoming part of the burgeoning punk scene. He played in several bands, but by his own admission, 'I wrote ballads but couldn't play an instrument properly.' Involvement in petty crime led to his arrest and a suspended sentence, after which Welsh changed the focus of his life. He worked for a local London council, studied computing and eventually returned to Edinburgh. All the time, he was experimenting with writing. Enamoured with the Beat writers and having experienced his own fair share of a world centred around drugs, he created a series of characters that would populate his short story collection *The Acid House* (1994) and *Trainspotting* (1993). But what made these tales so compelling was his extraordinary use of language and dialect. As Roddy Doyle captured the voice of working-class Dublin in his Barrytown stories, so Welsh mined a particular Scottish patter for his early books. They were scabrous, occasionally repulsive, frequently funny and guaranteed to outrage those easily shocked. That allegedly included two judges of the 1993 Booker Prize, who ensured the novel did not progress beyond the longlist.

Welsh returned to his *Trainspotting* characters with *Porno* (2002), while *Skagboys* (2012) presented a grimly funny portrait of the characters' early lives and *The Blade Artist* (2016) focused specifically on an older, but no less repentant, Begbie. Outside of that gang, characters are often reprised in different stories, with the combined novels presenting readers with an interconnected world. And if the uncompromisingly nihilistic *Filth* (1998) and its sequel *Crime* (2008) saw Welsh cross the legal divide, showing that the law was no less willing to indulge its darker side, *The Sex Lives of Siamese Twins* (2014) showed that the underbelly of Miami – where the author was living at the time – wasn't so different to the world of his blistering debut.

VIRGINIA WOOLF (1882–1941)

—— THE BOHEMIAN MODERNIST

Virginia Woolf became a dominant member of the Bloomsbury Group and was renowned for her ground-breaking fiction, her stance on women's position in society, vivid reminiscences of her youth and prolific letter writing.

Her life may have been beset with depression, which engulfed her in the period leading up to her suicide in a river near her Sussex home, but Woolf's writing thrilled with its invention, particularly her pioneering approach to stream of consciousness narrative. She was born Adeline Virginia Stephen, the third of four children, with four step-siblings from the previous marriages of Julia, once a Pre-Raphaelite artist's model, socialite and renowned philanthropist, and Leslie Stephen, a celebrated literary editor. The early deaths of her mother, step-sister and father, between 1895 and 1905, prompted a series of breakdowns that underpinned Woolf's precarious mental state throughout her life. It was compounded by the sexual abuse she was subjected to at a young age, which she wrote about in later life.

Although denied the formal education her brothers had had at Cambridge University, Woolf enjoyed access to private tutors and eminent academics. The family library was a vital resource, and the home frequently played host to some of the country's most engaged thinkers and artists. Through her brothers, Woolf and her sister Vanessa mingled with the 'Midnight Society', a circle of Cambridge students that included Clive Bell, Lytton Strachey and Leonard Woolf, who would all play a major role in the Bloomsbury Group and the sisters' personal lives.

While living in Kensington, Woolf had already begun to write. She created the 'Hyde Park Gate News', chronicling the activities of her large extended family, and began a life of letter writing. Summers while her parents were alive were spent in St Ives,

which inspired the novels *Jacob's Room* (1922), *To the Lighthouse* (1927) and *The Waves* (1931). Following her father's death, the family moved to Bloomsbury, which became the centre of artistic and intellectual gatherings. During this period, Woolf wrote anonymous reviews for publications such as the *Times Literary Supplement* and began to experiment with long-form fiction. Inspired by the new wave of artists that included Picasso and Cézanne, she envisaged a potential new path for the art of writing.

She married Leonard Woolf following his return from serving as a government administrator in Ceylon (now Sri Lanka). Their marriage was fluid, with both engaging in extra-marital relationships, most notably Virginia's with fellow writer Vita Sackville-

West, whose life inspired *Orlando*. In 1913, Woolf completed *The Voyage Out*, with characters loosely based on friends and family members. But insecurities drove her to another suicide attempt. She moved with Leonard to Richmond in 1914, remaining there for a decade, before returning to a house in Bloomsbury's Tavistock Square, which became the home of Hogarth Press, the publisher of Woolf's novels. Woolf wrote most of her major novels there, only moving to Sussex after the house had been destroyed by German bombers in the Blitz. That period in Bloomsbury was Woolf's most artistically intensive, developing a style and voice that saw her recognized as one of the 20th century's most significant writers.

66 WHEN I CANNOT SEE
WORDS CURLING LIKE RINGS
OF SMOKE ROUND ME I AM IN
DARKNESS – I AM NOTHING. **99**

THE WAVES

KEY WORKS

—

Kathy Acker

Great Expectations (1983)

Blood and Guts in High School (1984)

Empire of the Senseless (1988)

Also Read:

*The Childlike Life of the Black Tarantula
By the Black Tarantula* (1973)

Hannibal Lecter, My Father (1991)

Eve Babitz

Eve's Hollywood (1974)

*Slow Days, Fast Company: The World,
The Flesh, and L.A.* (1977)

*Sex and Rage: Advice to Young Ladies
Eager for a Good Time* (1979)

Also Read:

L.A. Woman (1982)

Black Swans (1993)

J.G. Ballard

The Atrocity Exhibition (1970)

Crash (1973)

Empire of the Sun (1984)

Also Read:

Vermillion Sands (1971, short stories)

Concrete Island (1974)

Super-Cannes (2000)

Djuna Barnes

Ryder (1928)

Nightwood (1936)

The Antiphon (1958, play)

Also Read:

*The Book of Repulsive Women: 8
Rhythms and 5 Drawings* (1915)

A Book (1921)

Charles Bukowski

Post Office (1971)

Factotum (1975)

Ham on Rye (1982)

Also Read:

*Poems Written Before Jumping out of
an Eight-Story Window* (1968, poetry)

Notes of a Dirty Old Man (1969, writings)

Women (1978)

Tales of Ordinary Madness (1983, short stories)

Mikhail Bulgakov

The Master and Margarita (1967)

Also Read:

The White Guard (1926)

A Country Doctor's Notebook (1975)

William Burroughs

Junkie (1953)

The Naked Lunch (1959)

The Soft Machine (1961/66)

Also Read:

Cities of the Red Night (1981)

The Place of Dead Roads (1983)

The Western Lands (1987)

Octavia E. Butler

Patternmaster (1976)

Parable of the Sower (1993)

Also Read:

Kindred (1979)

Parable of the Talents (1998)

Italo Calvino

Cosmicomics (1965, trans. 1968, short stories)

Invisible Cities (1972, trans. 1974)

If on a Winter's Night a Traveller (1979, trans. 1981)

Also Read:

Into the War (1954, trans. 2011)

Italian Folk Tales (1956, trans. 1961)

Mr. Palomar (1983, trans. 1985)

Albert Camus

The Outsider (1942)

The Plague (1947)

The Fall (1956)

Also Read:

The Myth of Sisyphus (1942)

Caligula (1944)

The Rebel (1951)

Angela Carter

The Magic Toyshop (1967)

The Bloody Chamber (1979, short stories)

Nights at the Circus (1984)

Also Read:

Heroes and Villains (1969)

Fireworks: Nine Profane Pieces
    (1974, short stories)

The Sadeian Woman and the
    Ideology of Pornography (1979)

Colette

Claudine at School (1900)

Chéri (1920)

Gigi (1944)

Also Read:

The Vagabond (1910)

The Last of Chéri (1926)

Looking Backwards (1941/42)

Maryse Condé

Heremakhonon (1976)

Segu (1987)

Only Tales From The Heart: True Stories From My Childhood (1998)

Also Read:

I, Tituba: Black Witch of Salem (1986)

Tree of Life (1992)

Windward Heights (1995)

Julio Cortázar

End of the Game and Other Stories
    (1956, short stories)

Hopscotch (1963)

62: A Model Kit (1968)

Also Read:

The Winners (1960)

A Manual for Manuel (1973)

Douglas Coupland

Generation X: Tales for an
    Accelerated Culture (1991)

Microserfs (1995)

All Families Are Psychotic (2001)

Also Read:

Girlfriend in a Coma (1998)

jPod (2006)

Worst. Person. Ever. (2013)

Philip K. Dick

The Man in the High Castle (1962)

Ubik (1969)

A Scanner Darkly (1977)

Also Read:

Do Androids Dream of Electric Sheep? (1968)

VALIS (1981)

Joan Didion

Slouching Towards Bethlehem (1968, essays)

Play It as It Lays (1970)

The Year of Magical Thinking (2005)

Also Read:

A Book of Common Prayer (1977)

The White Album (1979, essays)

Democracy (1984)

Marguerite Duras

The Sea Wall (1950, trans. 1952)

Moderato Cantabile (1958, trans. 1977)

The Lover (1984)

Also Read:

The Sailor from Gibraltar (1952, trans. 1966)

Hiroshima Mon Amour (1960, trans. 1961)

The North China Lover (1991, trans. 1992)

Ralph Ellison

Invisible Man (1952)

Shadow and Act (1964)

Also Read:

Juneteenth (1999)

*Living with Music: Ralph Ellison's
    Jazz Writings* (2002)

Elena Ferrante

My Brilliant Friend (2011, trans. 2012)

The Story of a New Name (2012, trans. 2013)

Those Who Leave and Those Who Stay
    (2013, trans. 2014)

The Story of the Lost Child
    (2014, trans. 2015)

Also Read:

The Days of Abandonment (2002, trans. 2005)

Fragments (2003, trans. 2016)

Janet Frame

A State of Siege (1966)

Living in the Maniototo (1979)

An Angel at My Table (1984)

Also Read:

Faces in the Water (1961)

The Carpathians (1989)

Jean Genet

Our Lady of the Flowers (1942, trans. 1943)

Querelle of Brest (1947, trans. 1953)

The Thief's Journal (1949)

Also Read:

Miracle of the Rose (1946, trans. 1951)

The Maids (1946, trans. 1947)

Funeral Rites (1947, trans. 1953)

Michel Houellebecq

Atomised (1998, trans. 2000)

Platform (2001, trans. 2002)

Serotonin (2019)

Also Read:

Lanzarote (2000, trans. 2002)

Submission (2015)

Zora Neale Hurston

Their Eyes Were Watching God (1937)

Moses, Man of the Mountain (1939)

Dust Tracks on a Road (1942)

Also Read:

Jonah's Gourd Vine (1934)

Seraph on the Suwanee (1948)

Denis Johnson

Jesus' Son (1992, short stories)

Tree of Smoke (2007)

Train Dreams (2011)

Also Read:

Angels (1983)

Resuscitation of a Hanged Man (1991)

Franz Kafka

The Metamorphosis (1915)

The Trial (1925)

The Castle (1926)

Also Read:

'The Judgement' (1912)

'In the Penal Colony' (1919)

Amerika (1927)

Ken Kesey

One Flew Over the Cuckoo's Nest (1962)

Sometimes a Great Notion (1964)

Also Read:

The Electric Kool-Aid Acid Test (Tom Wolfe, 1968)

Last Go Round (with Ken Babbs, 1994)

Chris Kraus

I Love Dick (1997)

Aliens and Anorexia (2000)

After Kathy Acker: A Biography (2017)

Also Read:

Torpor (2006)*Where Art Belongs* (2011)

Summer of Hate (2012)

Milan Kundera

The Joke (1967)

The Book of Laughter and Forgetting (1979)

The Unbearable Lightness of Being (1984)

Also Read:

The Art of the Novel (1986)

Immortality (1990)

Ignorance (2000)

Ursula K. Le Guin

A Wizard of Earthsea (1968)

The Left Hand of Darkness (1969)

The Dispossessed (1974)

Also Read:

The Lathe of Heaven (1971)

Catwings (1988)

Doris Lessing

The Grass is Singing (1950)

The Golden Notebook (1962)

Memoirs of a Survivor (1974)

Also Read:

*The Making of the Representative
    for Planet 8* (1982)

The Good Terrorist (1985)

Alfred and Emily (2008)

Cormac McCarthy

Blood Meridian (1985)

No Country for Old Men (2005)

The Road (2006)

Also Read:

Child of God (1973)

Suttree (1979)

All the Pretty Horses (1992)

Carson McCullers

The Heart is a Lonely Hunter (1940)

Reflections in a Golden Eye (1941)

The Member of the Wedding (1946)

Also Read:

*The Ballad of the Sad Café: The Novels
    and Stories of Carson McCullers*
    (1951, novella & short stories)

Illumination and Night Glare
    (1999, unfinished memoir)

Yukio Mishima

Forbidden Colors (1951)

The Temple of the Golden Pavilion (1956)

The Sea of Fertility (1965–70)

Also Read:

Thieves (1948)

Haruki Murakami

Norwegian Wood (1987)

The Wind-Up Bird Chronicle (1994–1995)

Kafka on the Shore (2002)

Also Read:

Dance, Dance, Dance (1988)

After the Quake (2000, short stories)

Underground (2000)

Anaïs Nin

House of Incest (1936)

Cities of the Interior (five volumes, 1959)

Collages (1964)

Also Read:

*D. H. Lawrence: An Unprofessional
    Study* (1932, non-fiction)

*Mirages: The Unexpurgated Diary
    of Anaïs Nin, 1939–1947* (2013, non-fiction)

*Trapeze: The Unexpurgated Diary
    of Anaïs Nin, 1947–1955* (2017, non-fiction)

Sylvia Plath

Ariel (1965, poetry collection)

The Bell Jar (1963)

Also Read:

The Colossus (1960, poetry collection)

Crossing the Water (1971, poetry collection)

Thomas Pynchon

V. (1963)

The Crying of Lot 49 (1966)

Gravity's Rainbow (1973)

Also Read:

Vineland (1990)

Mason & Dixon (1997)

Inherent Vice (2009)

Ayn Rand

The Fountainhead (1943)

Atlas Shrugged (1957)

Also Read:

We the Living (1936)

Anthem (1938)

*Introduction to Objectivist
    Epistemology* (1979, non-fiction)

Pauline Réage

Story of O (1954)

Jean Rhys

The Left Bank and Other Stories (1927)

Wide Sargasso Sea (1966)

Also Read:

Quartet (1928)

*Smile Please: An Unfinished
    Autobiography* (1979, memoir)

Juan Rulfo

El Llano en llamas (1953, short stories)

Pedro Páramo (1955)
Also Read:
The Golden Cockerel (1980)

Françoise Sagan

Bonjour Tristesse (1954)
Aimez-vous Brahms? (1959)
Also Read:
A Certain Smile (1956)
With Fondest Regards (1985)

J.D. Salinger

The Catcher in the Rye (1951)
Also Read:
Franny and Zooey (1961)
*Raise High the Roof Beam, Carpenters
    and Seymour: An Introduction* (1963)

Boris and Arkady Strugatsky

Noon: 22nd Century (1961)
Hard to Be a God (1964)
Roadside Picnic (1972)
Also Read:
The Dead Mountaineer's Inn (1970)
Monday Begins on Saturday (1965)

Jim Thompson

The Killer Inside Me (1952)
Savage Night (1953)
Pop. 1280 (1964)
Also Read:
Bad Boy (1953)
The Getaway (1958)
The Grifters (1963)

J.R.R. Tolkien

The Hobbit (1937)
The Lord of the Rings (1954–1955)
Also Read:
The Silmarillion (1977)

Kurt Vonnegut

Mother Night (1961)
Cat's Cradle (1963)
Slaughterhouse-Five (1969)
Also Read:
Player Piano (1952)
Bluebeard (1987)
Timequake (1997)

Irvine Welsh

Trainspotting (1993)
Filth (1998)
Porno (2002)
Also Read:
The Acid House (1994, short stories)
Marabou Stork Nightmares (1995)
Skagboys (2012)

Virginia Woolf

Mrs Dalloway (1925)
To the Lighthouse (1927)
Orlando: A Biography (1928)
Also Read:
A Room of One's Own (1929, essay)
The Waves (1931)
Between the Acts (1941)

INDEX

Ian Haydn Smith is a London-based writer. He is the update editor on *1001 Movies You Must See Before You Die* and is the editor of *BFI Filmmakers Magazine* and *Curzon Magazine*. Ian is also the author of *Selling the Movie: The Art of the Film Poster*, *The Short Story of Photography* and *Cult Filmmakers*.

Kristelle Rodeia is a freelance illustrator based in Paris. After studying Plastic Arts and Graphic Design, she is now a full time illustrator working in a mixture of pen, ink and digital drawings. Previous clients include *Stylist*, Veneta Bottega and *Erratum*.

Also in the Series:

CULT ARTISTS
CULT FILMMAKERS
CULT MUSICIANS

Brimming with creative inspiration, how-to projects and useful information to enrich your everyday life, Quarto Knows is a favourite destination for those pursuing their interests and passions. Visit our site and dig deeper with our books into your area of interest: Quarto Creates, Quarto Cooks, Quarto Homes, Quarto Lives, Quarto Drives, Quarto Explores, Quarto Gifts, or Quarto Kids.

First published in 2020 by White Lion Publishing, an imprint of The Quarto Group.
The Old Brewery, 6 Blundell Street,
London, N7 9BH,
United Kingdom
T (0)20 7700 6700
www.QuartoKnows.com

© 2020 Quarto Publishing plc.

Every effort has been made to trace the copyright holders of material quoted in this book. If application is made in writing to the publisher, any omissions will be included in future editions.

A catalogue record for this book is available from the British Library.

ISBN 978 0 71125 064 2
Ebook ISBN 978 0 71125 065 9

10 9 8 7 6 5 4 3 2 1

Design by Paileen Currie
Illustrations by Kristelle Rodeia

Printed in China